李怒
流沙即磐石
LI NU
AS IF SAND WERE STONE

TEXT BY NOOSHFAR AFNAN
文字　恩睦哲

Cornerstone Art

Holzwarth Publications

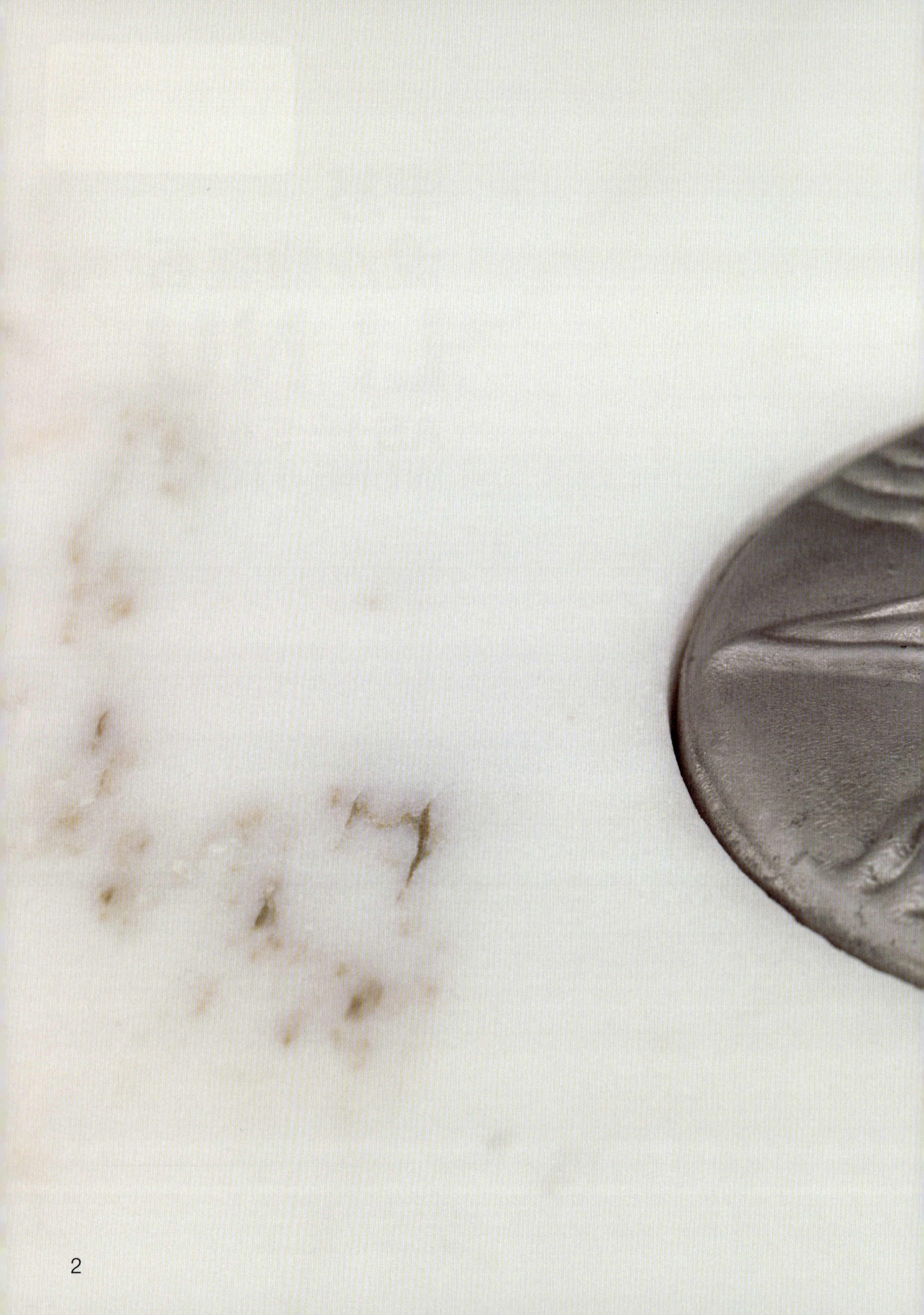

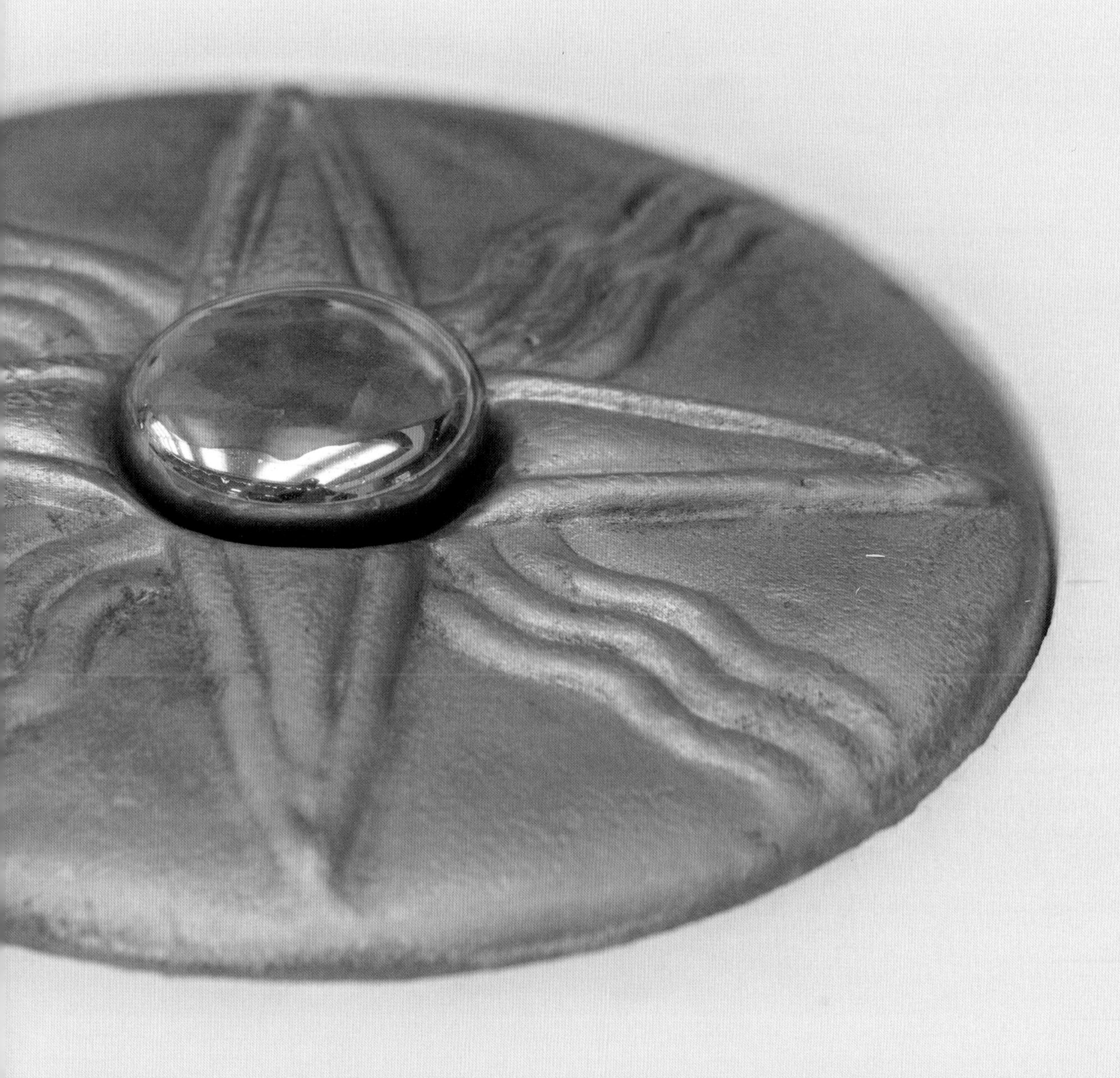

RE

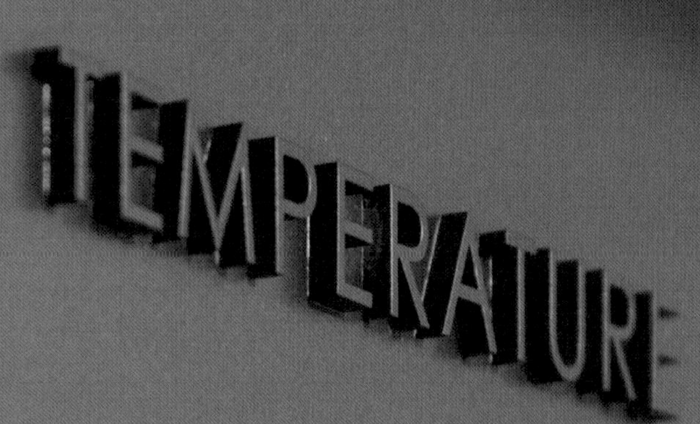

TEMPERATURE

NOOSHFAR AFNAN

READING LI NU

Introduction

Li Nu's first institutional solo exhibition at Today Art Museum coincided with the last and yet most intensive months of Covid-19 restrictions in China, the war in Ukraine and a world-wide economic downturn. The artist offers a novel commentary on the concerns and conditions of society, both in China and globally. He tackles such topics as personal freedom, societal values, the role of the individual in society and geopolitical tensions. He draws connections between East and West, be they in thought and philosophy or through a particular material, reminding us of the many areas of commonality between cultures. He showcases a dynamic body of work that is vastly diverse and yet highly cohesive, consisting of conceptual, text- and body-based sculptures and video works. Though each piece is unique, they all subtly and overtly engage with the rest of the show to offer a unified body of work.

Midway into their artistic careers, many artists begin to follow a recognisable style, a predictable pattern. Or they become known for using a certain medium or material; a particular visual vocabulary becomes associated with them. This kind of predictability or familiarity can delight us as viewers: It allows us to 'name that artist' at first glance of a new work. Li Nu denies us this comfort and instead challenges us to continually learn a new vernacular with each piece, to engage afresh with his work.

Words, Words, Words

Words matter to Li Nu. He chooses them carefully and intentionally, be it for the titles of his exhibitions and artworks or for use in text-based installations. Ideas from philosophy, literature and song lyrics wind elegantly and effortlessly through his body of work. As one of the conceptual artists of his generation who had the benefit of both an Eastern and a Western art education—currently based in Beijing, he received an MA in sculpture from the Royal College of Art in London—Li Nu relates his works with ease to literature and philosophy of both Asian and Euro-American origins.

The title of his show at Today Art Museum is inspired by a quote from Argentine writer Jorge Luis Borges: 'Nothing is built on stone; all is built on sand; but we must build as if the sand were stone.'[1] The artist reminds us that Borges's line is similar to Zen and Chinese philosophy, according to which a grain of sand is believed to hold the universe.[2] A grain of sand is the smallest unit of a stone, but it sustains pressure better than the stone.[3] The significance of this line of poetry is perhaps that no matter how uncertain and turbulent their situation in the world, by participating in society every individual can manifest rock-like qualities such as resilience and steadfastness.

The words of the large text-based installation that greets visitors on the tall red-brick exterior wall of the Today Art Museum have also been carefully chosen: 'WHAT'S THE DATE

TODAY?' (all works 2022 unless otherwise stated) is fashioned out of large stainless-steel letters, not only referencing the museum's name but also purposefully using the concept of date as a reminder that time is ticking even as society seems to fail to progress, or even moves backward. It is a reminder of our tumultuous past, uncertain present and the brighter future that we all yearn to envision. The Chinese title of this work (今夕是何年, Jīn xī shì hé nián) is a sentence borrowed from a poem by Northern Song Dynasty–era writer and calligrapher Sū Shì (1037–1101). It is intended to be sung to the 'Water Melody' (水调歌头, Shuǐdiào Gētóu) and translates to 'what year is it tonight'. Li Nu switched the word 'year' with 'date', based on the ancient saying that 'one day in heaven is one year on earth'. And he relates it to a few other lines further down in the poem speaking of people's 'sorrows, joys, parting and reunion': though 'a thousand miles apart, together [we see] the moon's beauty'. Li Nu wants us to show empathy toward the many current crises faced by every individual in the world.

Similarly, words—in the form of lyrics for a song—become the title of the installation *Spirit on the Water*, displayed in a window of the exhibition hall of the Today Art Museum. The title is taken from the title of a love song written by American singer-songwriter Bob Dylan, which in turn references a passage from the Bible's *Book of Genesis*. Against a backdrop of bright yellow, we see four chairs with their legs stuck to the wall, their seats visibly scorched. On the ground are scattered eight old glass buoys for fishing. The work reminds us of travel plans that have been on hold for too long or never materialised and rivers of people that no longer flow.

Text-based installations are another indication of the artist's interest in language as a form of artistic expression. In the work *Warm/September*, the word 'warm', spelled out with nickel-chrome wire, intermittently glows red-hot in a dark room. There is a gap in the wire before the last letter, so an alternate reading of 'war' is possible. Whereas we expect 'warm' to feel comfortably balmy, 'war' should be scorching hot and so uncomfortable as to burn our skin. In fact, if we could get any closer to this work, our skin would indeed burn: Li Nu has constructed a half-wall to protect the audience from the strong heat. Still, we feel not only the physical heat of the piece but the deep-burning anguish caused by ongoing global wars that wreak terror and suffering upon all of us in varying degrees of intensity.

References to Western literature can be found in the work *Ball of Fat*, a cubic installation filled with mutton fat. It is named after a character in an eponymous novella by French writer Guy de Maupassant, a 'coquette', or prostitute, who is described as 'small, round and fat'.[4] She turns out to have the noblest character of a group of carriage passengers who are fleeing their enemy during war. Not only does she share all the provisions she has brought, but, when they are held hostage, makes the ultimate sacrifice: Ball-of-Fat agrees to satisfy the physical urges of the enemy soldier. After her act of sacrifice, everyone is back in the carriage, but no one acknowledges Ball-of-Fat's presence or offers her any of their food. They 'first sacrificed her and then rejected her', Maupassant writes.[5] If, in Li's visual vocabulary, mutton fat stands for people, then it is a symbol for scores of workers and businesses who, during the pandemic, were abandoned and discarded once their services were no longer needed.

Li Nu is an admirer of Jean-Paul Sartre's writings, as evidenced by several works inspired by the French writer and philosopher in the upstairs hall. The sound installation *Fly*, for instance, was inspired by Sartre's 1943 play *The Flies*.[6] In the installation, we hear the buzzing sound of a fly while we walk through a darkened room. The theme continues visually with *Why Can't I Have Both Angels and Demons Kiss Me?*, an oil-on-canvas painting depicting two large flies facing in opposite directions, their bodies and wings touching. The title is perhaps a reference to the idea that the difference between good or evil, right or wrong, is not always easy to define. Flies are generally regarded as pesky little insects, but in ancient Egypt, for instance, they were held in high regard.[7]

Placed directly across from *Why Can't I Have Both Angels and Demons Kiss Me?* is the bronze sculpture *The Painful Secret of Gods and Kings*, which, in its diptych composition, mimics the two flies of the painting. The title—also taken from Sartre's *The Flies*—continues semantically around the back of the sculpture: The word 'LIBERTY' is engraved in capital letters on each portion of a halved stone, once normally and once in reverse. Lastly, the small white marble installation *Exit* is an homage to Sartre's 1944 popular play *No Exit*, which deals with a trio of damned souls' vexed relationships while stuck together in hell. The work consists of a small milky-white marble box that is punched with holes reading 'exit' in inverted braille. Atop the box are nestled two small golden flies. If one gets too close, the work emits the sound of an electric shock. Only when the viewer changes their position can they see the braille word 'exit' written in the correct way, as reflected in the mirror behind it. The Chinese title of the work, 死亡是唯一的出口 (Sǐwáng shì wéiyī de chūkǒu), is telling: It translates to 'Death Is the Only Exit'.

Another recurring feature in Li Nu's oeuvre is the use of puns. *In Gold We Trust*—which riffs on the American expression engraved into U.S. currency, 'In God We Trust'—is a work that consists of three large bronze sculptures in the shape of bent coins that are blown up to mythical proportions. According to the artist, the work is also inspired by the novel *The Moon and Sixpence* (1919) by British novelist W. Somerset Maugham, in which the author examines the idea that 'people often forget the sixpence at their feet when they look up at the moon'.[8] For Maugham, the moon stands for the ideal realm of art and beauty while the sixpence stands for the world of reality and human relationships. Bridging East and West, Li Nu relates this quote to Buddhist texts, in which the moon stands for truth and the finger is only a tool for pointing at truth.[9] The Lankavatara Sutra says: 'As the ignorant grasp the fingertip and not the moon, so those who cling to the letter know not my truth.'[10]

Tellingly, the artist chose to enlarge the smallest unit of three random currencies, and mostly erased identifying marks. For the one based on a U.S. coin, he replaced 'God' with 'Gold'. The phrase 'In Gold We Trust' sets up the question: What happens in societies when we no longer trust and rely on a divine or supreme being? Li Nu suggests that our material culture reflects our values. In a society that does not value any higher good or divine power, money, labour and people tend to be perceived as purely transactional—a hellscape straight out of a Sartre play.

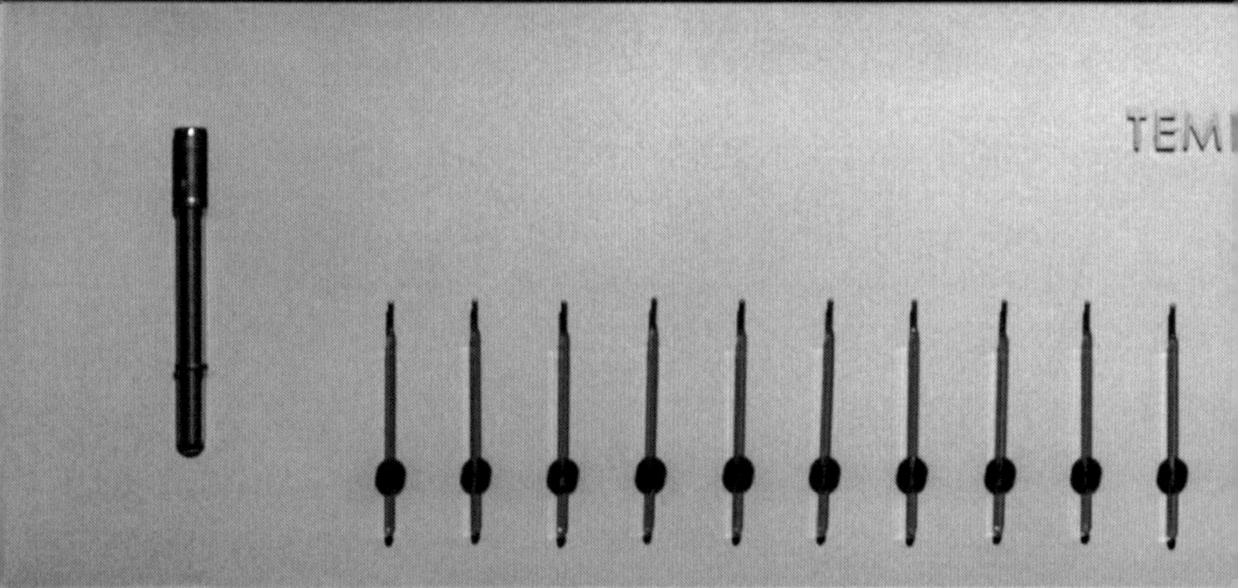

TEM

URE

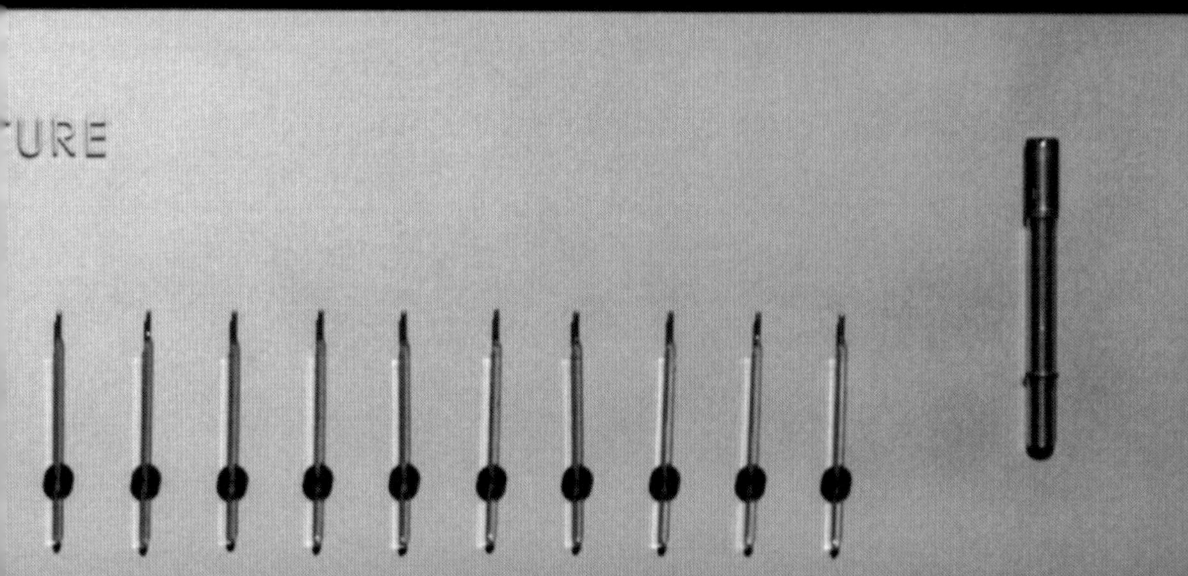

Media + Material = Message

While the choice of materials and media is vital in conveying the message in any artwork, Li Nu's oeuvre is remarkable in its wide range of materials: from the unconventional, such as sheep tallow, beeswax and mercury, to more traditional materials, including marble and bronze. Although trained as a sculptor, he goes far beyond traditional sculpture in his range of media: There are text-based works, sound installations, a video and a painting in this exhibition, as if expressing the complexity of the world we live in requires a larger variety of materials than a single medium can contain.

Li Nu's practice demonstrates a particular care in his selection of materials. In making *Pillar Imperfect*, for instance, the artist was shown four different choices of stone before he found an acceptable medium. The smoothly polished white marble he chose has been shaped into an 11-sided column. The Chinese name for this stone, 汉白玉 (hàn báiyù), connotes 'white jade', which implies delicacy and luminosity. But he shaped it after Fort Wood, the massive pedestal of the Statue of Liberty in New York, which was ironically once used as a military fort. Inside this stone, he has placed an aluminium pillar, measuring 10 cm in diameter. A glass ball enclosed with mercury caps the column with a decorative disc. Should the glass break and the mercury be allowed to fuse with the aluminium, a process called 'flocculation' would occur: Clumps of large flakes would build up, creating a messily degraded mass that would look like a crude reproduction of the Statue of Liberty.

The choice of mercury, a rather unusual material with numerous symbolic associations, further distinguishes this sculpture. Mercury is unique as the only metal that is liquid at room temperature. It is both a poison (as mercury vapour is highly toxic) and used as a medicine. It is also an element connected to both Eastern and Western societies; in China it is considered the original Taoist alchemical elixir. After extensive research, experts have concluded that there is a large amount of the element in the tomb of Qínshǐhuáng, the founder of the Qin dynasty who ruled from 221 to 210 BC. It served several purposes: to embalm the body, to act as an anti-corrosion agent and to prevent theft.[11] Perhaps Li Nu likes the ambivalence that this duality of meanings presents: Is the mercury assisting or sabotaging the construction of the pillar?

The use of mercury connects with another work in the show: the small installation *Thermometer*, which contains a row of the titular instruments. Thermometers are democratic: They are found in every household and generally considered reliable. However, during the pandemic, they were used to curb liberty: An outlier test result denied citizens access to enter the supermarket, ride public transport or go to school and work. In Li's thermometers, instead of providing a temperature reading the mercury rises in accordance to 'THE MEASURE OF LIBERTY': The degree markings have been replaced with these words.

As mentioned in our discussion of *Ball of Fat*, another unusual material that plays an important role in several of Li Nu's works is mutton fat. The artist began to use the material in 2019 while working on the massive site-specific installation *Iron Curtain*, set on the border between China and Mongolia. A cast was built, to be filled with water, which then would freeze and become a massive wall of ice more than two metres high, almost a me-

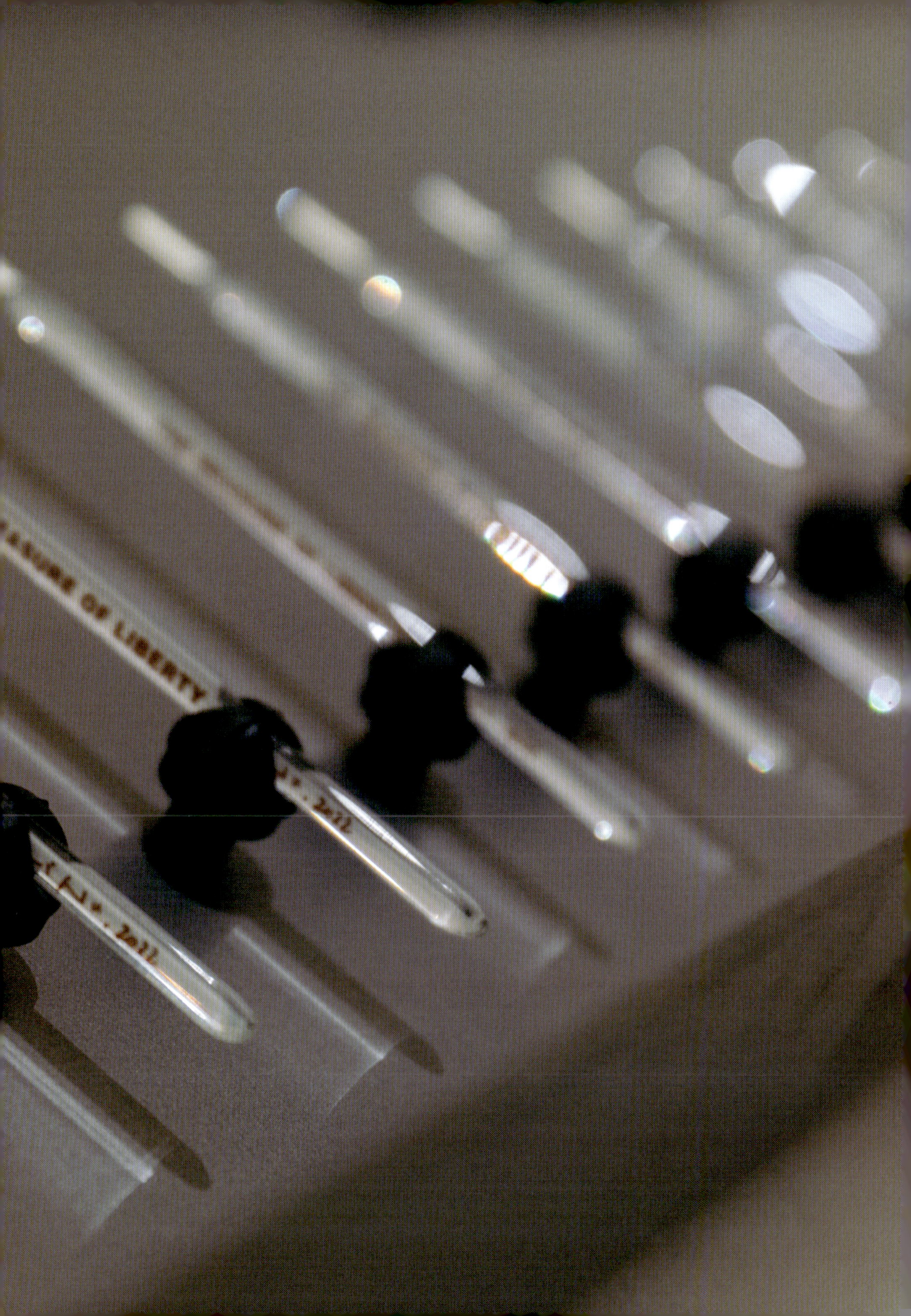

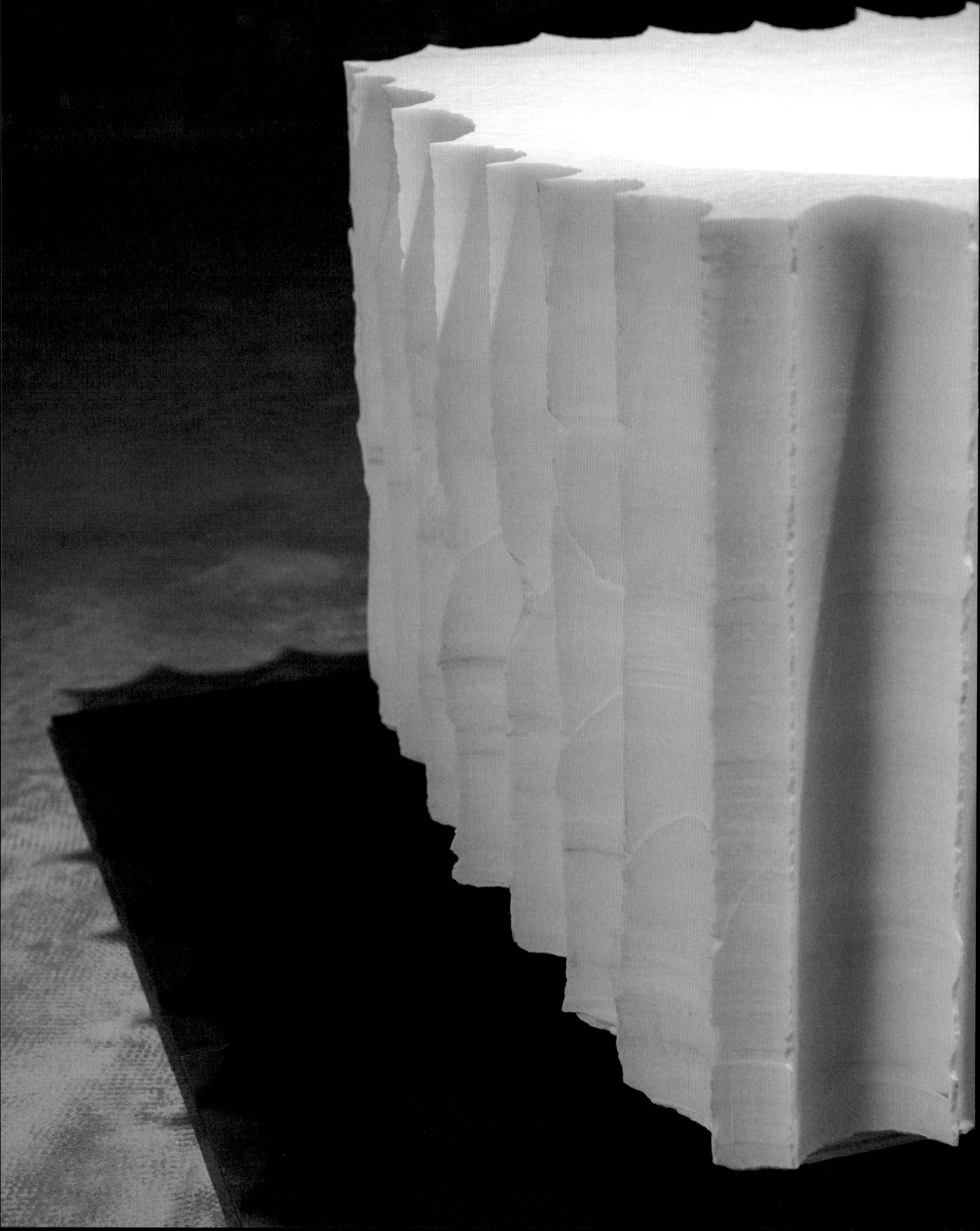

tre wide and 36 metres long. When the cast began to leak, the local herdsmen suggested that the artist use mutton fat to close any gaps in the structure. It worked. Li Nu cast another wall on a smaller scale in the work *Air on the G String* (2021) during his solo exhibition *Peace Piece* at SPURS Gallery in 2021. For that work, however, the cast was entirely filled with around 16 tonnes of mutton fat. For *Ball of Fat*, the artist collected the seals of businesses that no longer exist. The small seals protrude through the mass of fat that, as Li Nu states, 'form… a scab-like wound on the surface'.[12] These businesses were swallowed during the economic maelstrom of the pandemic, severely impacting many livelihoods. Each company seal represents a failed business that in turn affected hundreds or more people, as symbolised by the mass of surrounding fat.

Another unusual material Li Nu uses is beeswax. At the Today Art Museum, it is the medium of six life-sized human statues. Collectively titled *Waterfall*, each figure is modelled after the artist's own body. One senses vulnerability in their posture: They lean against the wall, their arms folded over their heads, exposing the soft flesh of their backs. The malleability of beeswax—its potential for deforming and melting—further enhances the frailty of the figures. They connect with works such as *Warm/September*, *Pillar Imperfect* and *Thermometer* in the visceral connection between themes such as 'body', 'heat' and 'temperature'. Li Nu's usage of unusual materials extends to the everyday. In *If You See Her, Say Hello* (another title taken from a Bob Dylan lyric) the artist uses two different-sized rubberized cotton raincoats with hoods. They are hung facing one another, implying an intimate conversation or tête-à-tête that the viewer is free to imagine for themselves. Formally, this installation also reverses the orientation of the aforementioned oil painting *Why Can't I Have Both Angels and Demons Kiss Me?*, in which the silhouettes of two flies face in opposite directions, their bodies and wings touching.

Through this great diversity of materials Li Nu forges a cohesive and unified body of work that allows his messaging to reverberate across various topics.

Body, Me, We

For any artist, their body is their most easily accessible medium. Li Nu uses his own body as a point of departure for many of his works, including durational performances, videos and sculptures. His use of the corporeal stems not only from convenience, however; it is a tool to elicit a common understanding, shared experience or sense of empathy from his viewers. Rather than addressing his individual self and ego, he is appealing to our common humanity, our shared understanding.

As mentioned above, the six life-size sculptures *Waterfall* are based on moulds of the artist's body. In their soft-wax medium and vulnerability of posture, they elicit empathy from the audience. Notably, each of the six sculptures has a torch tip nozzle protruding out of a body part, which nods both to the sculptures' making and our own reproduction as a species.

The theme of navels—our bodies' mark of birth—can be found in a collection of works that share the title *Mundus*, 'the world' in Latin. The centrepiece of this work is a large block of white marble with an enlarged navel carved after a mould of the artist's own,

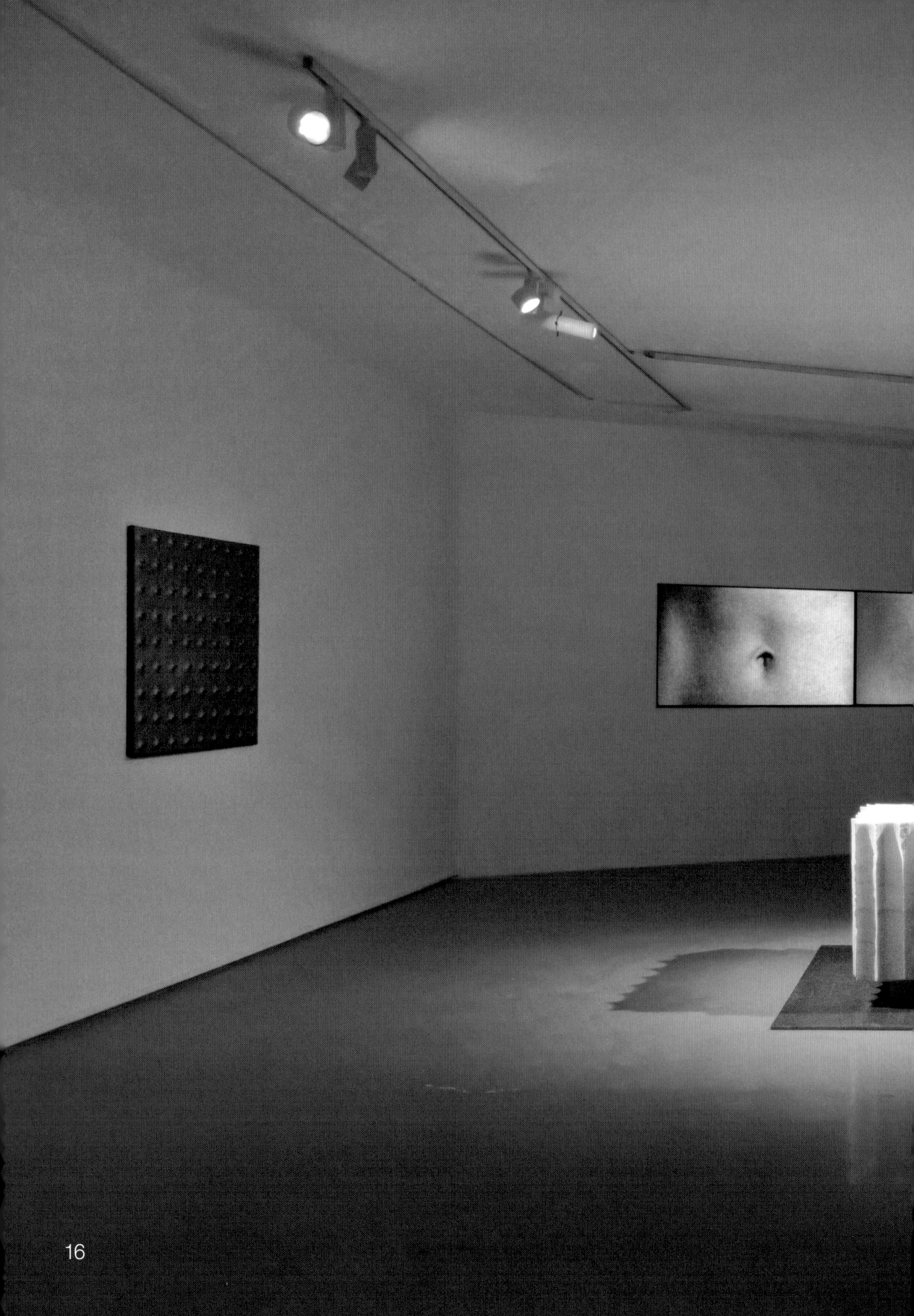

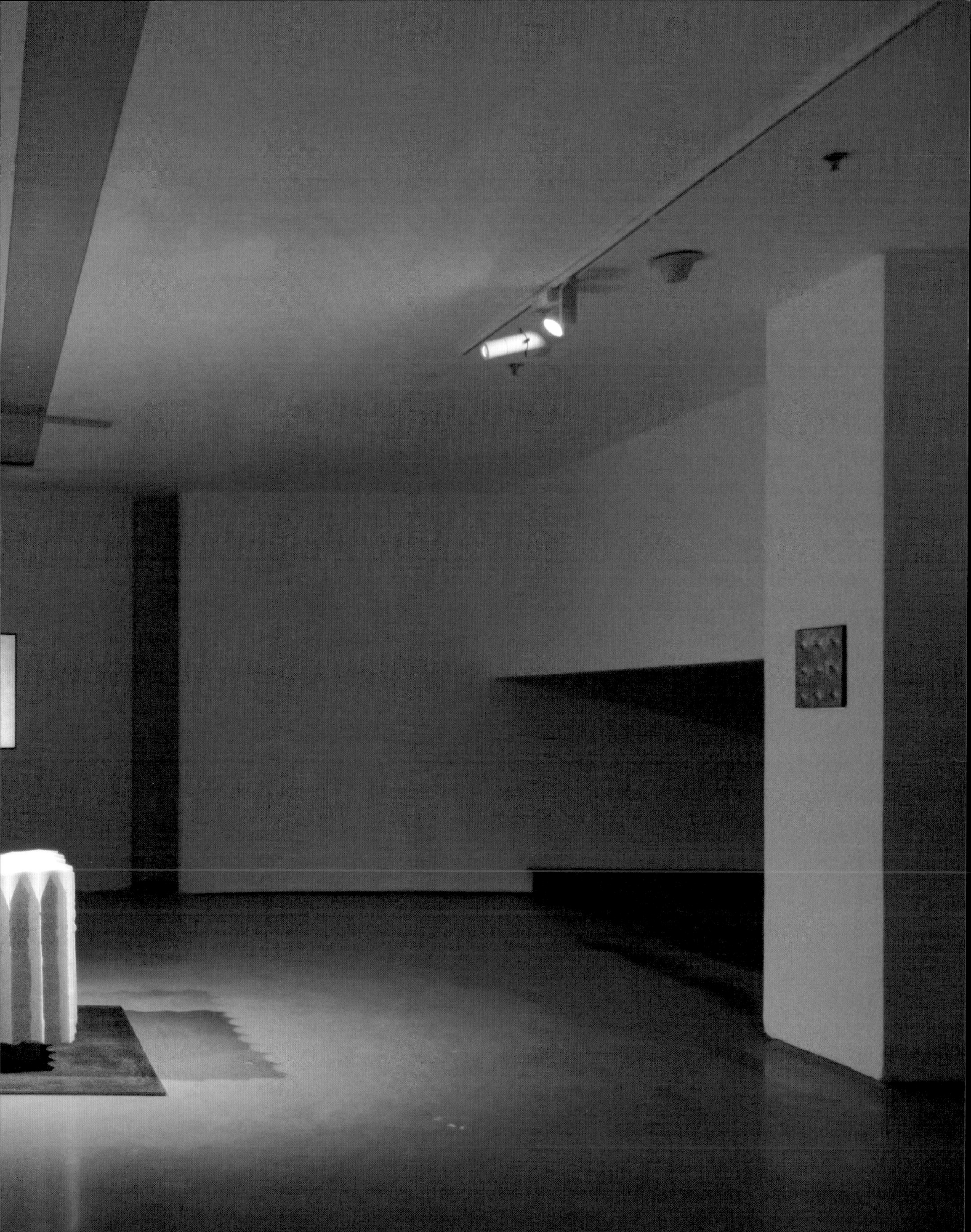

its centre facing upwards, hinting at a recumbent figure. Li Nu connects the idea for this sculpture to a practice in ancient Rome in which a hole was dug to symbolise the connection of the underground gods with those of the sky. The supine position suggests a different viewpoint from the standing position from which we typically see the world.[13]

Nearby, a short video work projects on two screens: a navel on each, or one navel juxtaposed with a back, as the model moves slowly back and forth. For Li Nu, this is symbolic of 'the original relationship between man and the world'.[14] Lastly, the artist's negative casts of his navel protrude like thorns from two flat bronze plates. In English, the expression 'navel gazing' refers to a preoccupation with oneself: seeing oneself and one's concern at the centre of the universe. In fact, what Li Nu is doing is the opposite: He offers a universal symbol, the origin of life, something that all humans share and can identify with. Both the positioning of the navel in these sculptures—the suggestion of a recumbent body in the marble sculpture, as well as using reverse casts of the navel—point to the idea of viewing things from a new or different perspective. For Li Nu, the bronze sculptures are 'a symbol of decentralisation and the plurality of centres'.[15] There is room, the artist suggests, for multiple centres or points of origin to exist concurrently: Every nation should be allowed to be its own centre.

Li Nu engages not only his own body in these works, but also those of the members of the audience, who must navigate through the exhibition in uncommon ways and experience strong attacks on their bodily senses. Two hanging walls in the show require the audience to duck and move under them to get to the next space. These spatial interventions induce a sense of anticipation in the viewer, which the artist explains by using the common Chinese idiom 先抑后扬 (xiānyì hòuyáng), meaning 'first putting someone down and then raising them up'.[16] At the entrance of the show, a hanging wall leads to the work *Pillar Imperfect*. On the lower edge of this wall the artist has added the line, 'Are the eyebrows your feathers?' This argues that our eyebrows are a most expressive feature of our body—especially while wearing a face mask.[17] A second hanging wall inhibits immediate access to the text-based installation *Warm/September*. Once we enter the space and stand in front of a half-wall, the work not only engages our vision but our sense of touch, causing us to experience fiery heat on our skin.

Another spatial intervention is found in the upstairs hall in *Asylum*, an installation in four acts, where steel-mesh partition walls divide the large space into four distinct areas, obliging the viewer to move from space to space in a particular order that represents, to Li Nu, the states of a person's mind.[18]

Next, our auditory senses are assaulted in the large installation *All That Is Solid Melts into Air* (2019). As the audience steps onto the expansive raised platform of steel plates, an unexpected and deafening gunshot sounds, instilling an immediate sense of fear, panic and concern for the well-being of others. In contrast is the very quiet but continuous sound of the audio installation *Fly*, discussed above. Here, however, the darkness of the room creates a sense of discomfort and suspense.

Lastly, *Exit* emits the sound of an electric shock, causing our bodies to experience a small jolt. As is evident from the works discussed, besides offering a rich visual feast for our eyes, this show also intensely stimulates our senses of touch and hearing. As the body is the one medium that the artist shares with each member of the audience, it becomes a potent tool to convey his message: It concurrently represents the most individual of experience while underlining the similarities between us all. His use of the body reminds us of our oneness: Our destinies are all closely interwoven.

Unpacking the 'Centre'

The idea of the 'centre' features prominently in *Mundus*. While doing research on this work, Li Nu realised that the idea of a single origin or centre is prevalent in the visual history of many cultures, as well as religious and spiritual traditions. The idea of the centre, for example, is described by scholar Titus Burckhardt in relation to several faith traditions. Among the Sioux people of North America, a fire altar was ceremoniously created that acknowledged the four directions, the earth and the sky. The altar was seen as 'the centre of the world, and this centre, which in reality is everywhere, is the dwelling-place of the Great Spirit'.[19] Because this point was seen to be everywhere, 'a symbolical reference is sufficient for its realisation'.[20] In the ancient Chinese tradition of Taoist art, a disc perforated in the middle, often made of jade, was a commonly seen emblem. 'The disc represents the heavens or the cosmos,' Burkhardt writes, 'and the void in the centre the unique and transcendent Essence.'[21] And in the Christian tradition, God is described thus: 'He is the all, He is the beginning, the end, and the timeless centre.'[22] Rudolf Arnheim offers another angle to approach the discussion of a 'centre'—a theory of visual composition around two basic spatial patterns, one of which he terms concentric or cosmic centre.[23] *Mundus* exhibits the importance of the 'centre' from both a formal and a conceptual point of view. In his own statement about the series, Li Nu points us to the Roman architect and engineer Vitruvius (c. 75–c. 15 BC)[24], who wrote in *De Architectura* or *The Ten Books on Architecture* about the proportion of man. He explains that if the arms and legs are extended, one can circumscribe the human with the navel as the centre. Within that circle, a square can be drawn from the head to the feet and across the fully extended arms.[25] During the Renaissance, his work was taken up by architects, artists and engineers—including Leonardo da Vinci, who derived his famous Vitruvian Man from this diagrammatic image. Li Nu also mentions the Roman method of mapping the centre point of a city before construction began—this midpoint was called the 'mundus', the aforementioned point of connection between the city and the gods, both underground and in heaven. He concludes his research-based introduction to the *Mundus* works: 'Legend has it that Romulus founded Rome by excavating a "world" on the Palatine hills on April 21, 753 BC.'

Li Nu explains his intention with the *Mundus* video, which depicts the back and navel of a model in gentle motion: He intends the work to 'to clarify the original connection between human beings and nature, cities and the world'. The navel, he writes, 'is the centre of human beings; it is also the centre of the world, human beings are the world.'[26]

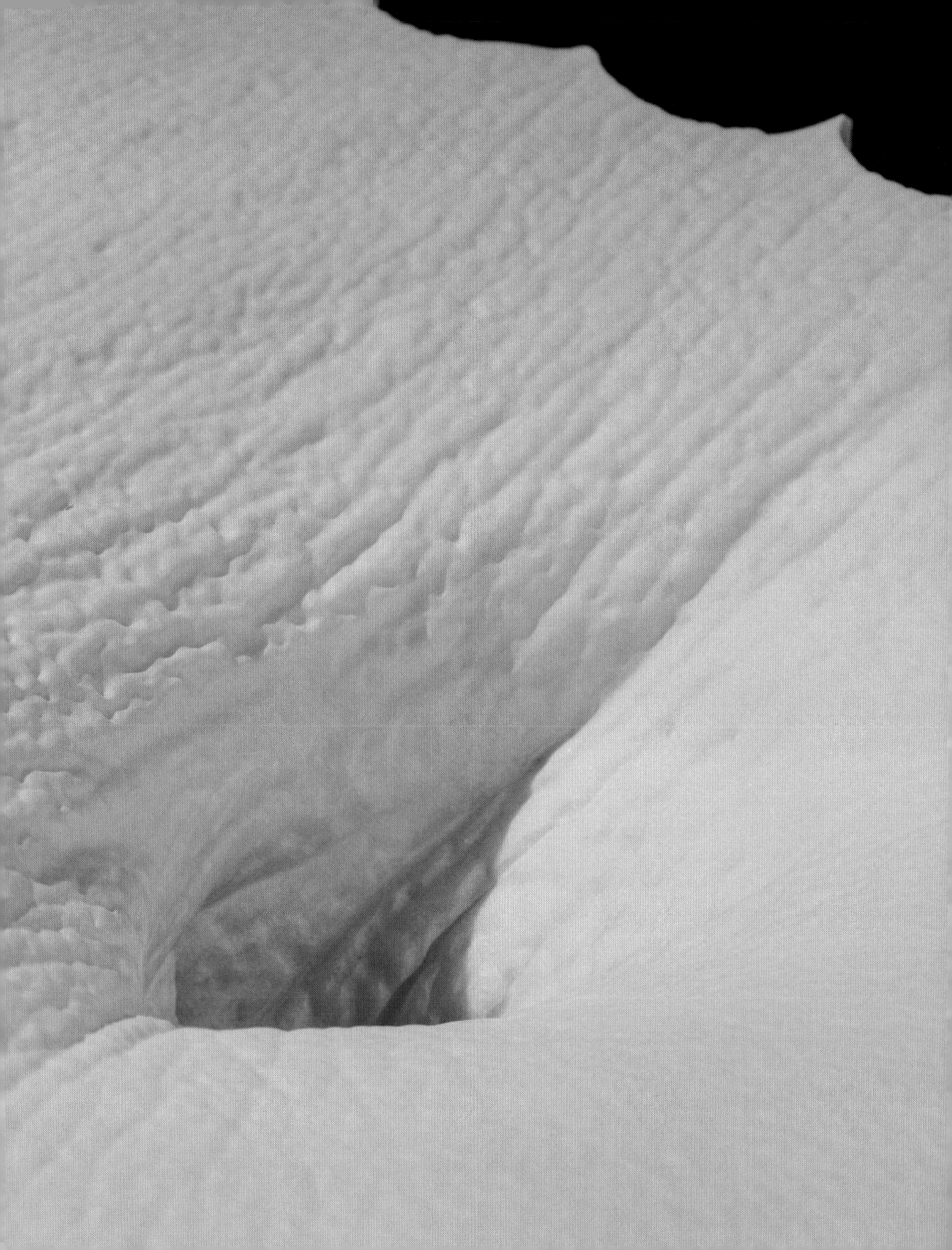

Conclusion

In his first institutional show, Li Nu offers us a large body of work rich in visual vocabulary and diverse in the use of media and materials, not just as a visual feast, but also eliciting a response from our senses of hearing and touch. He offers alternative and unexpected ways of viewing the socio-political issues facing people everywhere. Although it is difficult to pin down Li Nu's art to a specific style or medium in this show, there are elements of importance that recur: words—whether inspired by literature, lyrics or puns, whether appearing in the form of text-based works, the exhibition title or titles of works—are a fundamental aspect of Li Nu's body of work and a crucial part of his messaging. They afford the artist opportunities to either juxtapose or make connections between overlapping ideas found in Eastern and Western philosophy. Uncommon as well as traditional media allow for a depth and breadth of expression rich in symbolism. His use of the body—specifically, *his* body—as a starting point of several works allows for a realisation of the universal: the things that bind us together as humans. Finally, he draws on the importance of the 'centre', a powerful symbol since ancient times found across different cultures and traditions, not only formally but also conceptually. Through these four pillars, Li Nu forges a body of work that draws upon and reflects universal concerns in our fraught age.

[1] From the poem titled 'From an Apocryphal Gospel'. The first published translation reads: 'Nothing is built upon rock: for all is built upon sand: but let each man build as if sand were rock…' *In Praise of Darkness*, trans. by Norman Thomas di Giovanni (London: Allen Lane, 1975), p. 111. Borges's poem seems to be a playful satire on the well-known verse 'blessed are the meek' from the Bible's *Gospel of Matthew* (5:5). [2] Li Nu in Zhi Shizhe, interview, 'Li Nu: Laizi Jijing de Jianzheng', Yiwenli *EACH*, posted 11-11-2022 (WeChat). [3] Li Nu in conversation with author. [4] https://en.wikisource.org/wiki/The_Complete_Short_Stories_of_Guy_de_Maupassant/Ball-of-Fat. [5] Ibid. [6] *The Flies*, in turn, was adapted from the Ancient Greek myth of Electra. [7] Li Nu in conversation with author. [8] Li Nu, artist's statement on *In Gold We Trust*. [9] Ibid. [10] 'The Lankavatara Sutra', ch. 6, p.193, translated by DT Suzuki (e-version) [11] https://terracottaarmychina.com/is-there-really-mercury-in-the-underground-palace-of-qin-shihuangs-mausoleum. [12] Li Nu in Zhi Shizhe, 'Li Nu: Laizi Jijing de Jianzheng'. [13] Li Nu, artist statement on the *Mundus* series. [14] Li Nu in Zhi Shizhe, 'Li Nu: Laizi Jijing de Jianzheng'. [15] Ibid. [16] Ibid. [17] Li Nu in conversation with author. [18] Li Nu, artist statement for *Asylum*. [19] As quoted in Titus Burckhardt, 'The Universality of Sacred Art', *The Essential Titus Burckhardt: Reflections on Sacred Art, Faiths, and Civilizations*, ed. by William Stoddart (Bloomington: World Wisdom, 2003), p. 97. [20] Ibid., p. 98. [21] Ibid., p. 105. [22] Ibid., p. 111. [23] *The Power of the Center: A Study of Composition in the Visual Arts* (1982). The second being the Cartesian or grid system. [24] Li Nu, artist statement on the *Mundus* series. [25] See Marcus Vitruvius Pollio, *De Architectura*, Book III, ch. 1.3, https://penelope.uchicago.edu/Thayer/E/Roman/Texts/Vitruvius/3*.html. [26] Li Nu, artist statement on the *Mundus* series.

Nooshfar Afnan is a writer and curator based in Toronto. While living in Beijing between 2005 and 2023, she contributed numerous reviews, artist interviews and feature articles to publications such as *frieze*, *ArtAsiaPacific* and *ARTOMITY*, focusing on contemporary art from China. She has been actively following Li Nu's work since 2017. She currently contributes to BIPOC art-focused magazine *Rungh*. She is the English editor of Jiang, Tao and Edward W., *A Story of Father and Son*, Hebei Fine Arts Publishing House, 2023, and co-author with Joe Carter of *The Baha'i House of Worship: Design, Construction and Community*, George Ronald Publisher, Oxford 2022. Catalogue essays include 'Feng Lianghong "Forest Hills"', N3 Gallery, Beijing 2022; 'Farley Aguilar: History Beckons', SPURS Gallery, Beijing 2021; 'Harmony and the Test of Time: Xiang Yang's Transfiguration House at the Echigo-Tsumari Art Triennale, Japan', 2018. She curated *Feng Zhijia: Psychedelic Iteration*, EGG Gallery, Beijing 2023, and co-curated, with Gao Yi, Christina Kubisch's *Electrical Walks – Shanghai*, UN Art Center, Shanghai 2018.

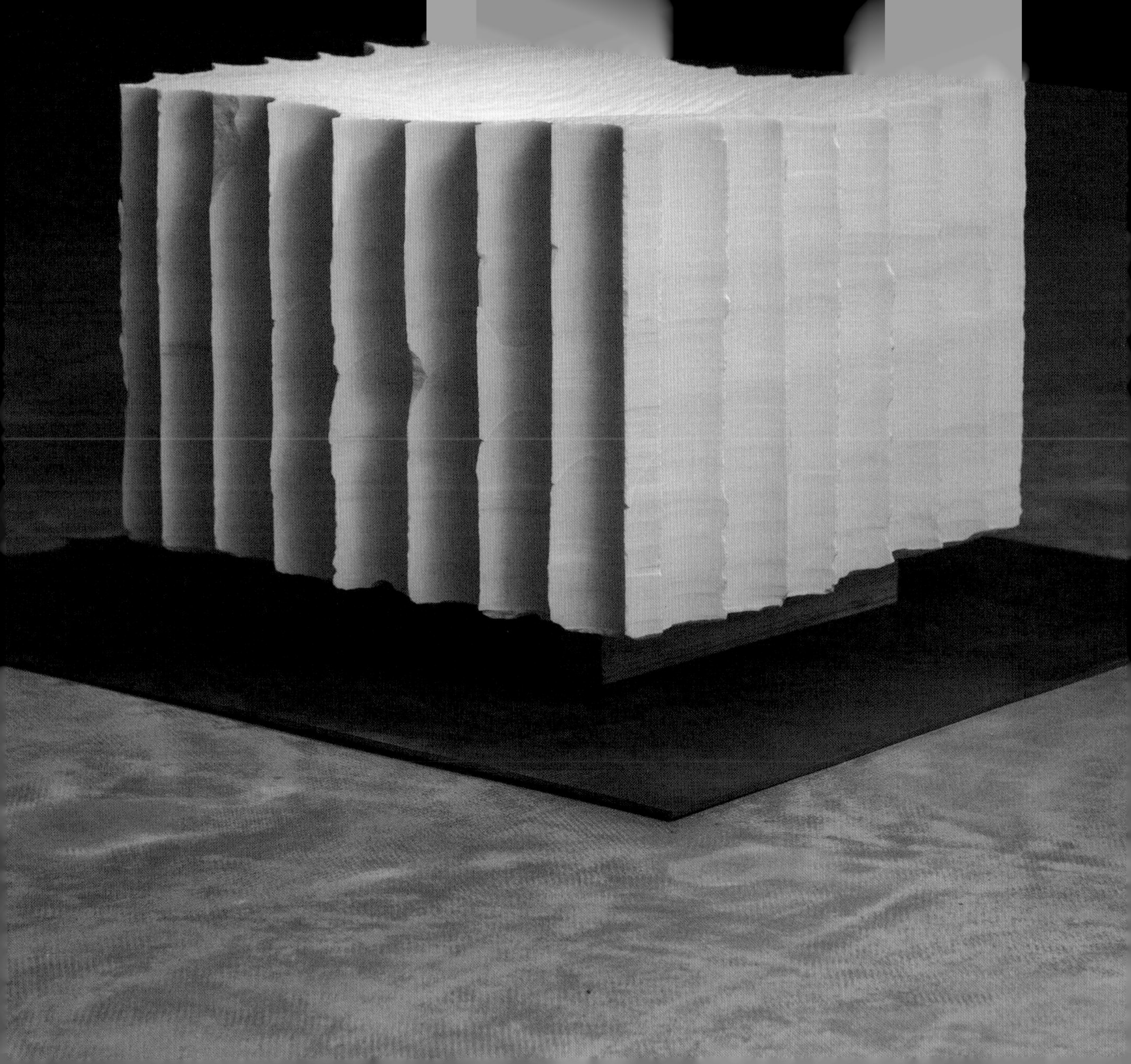

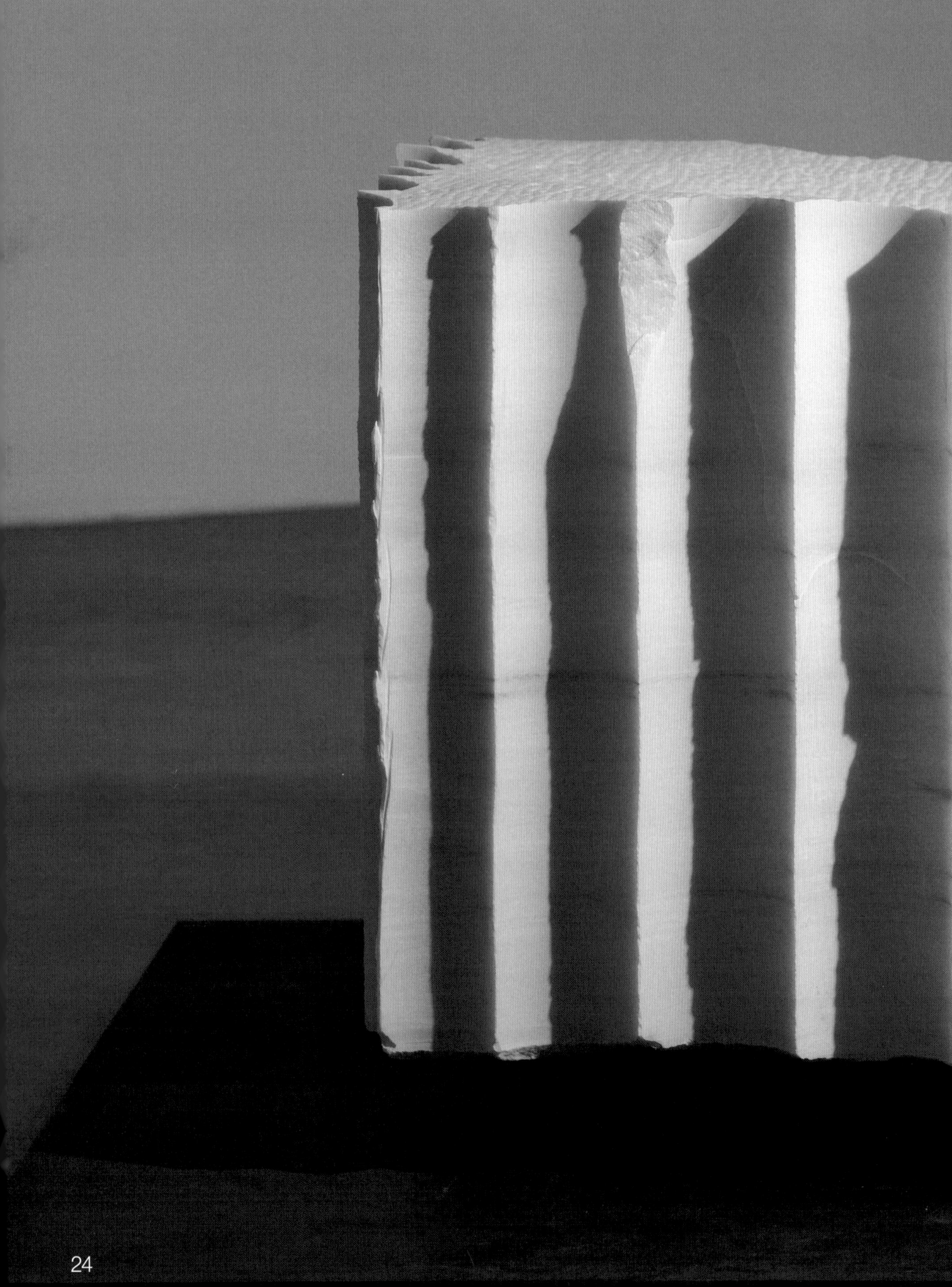

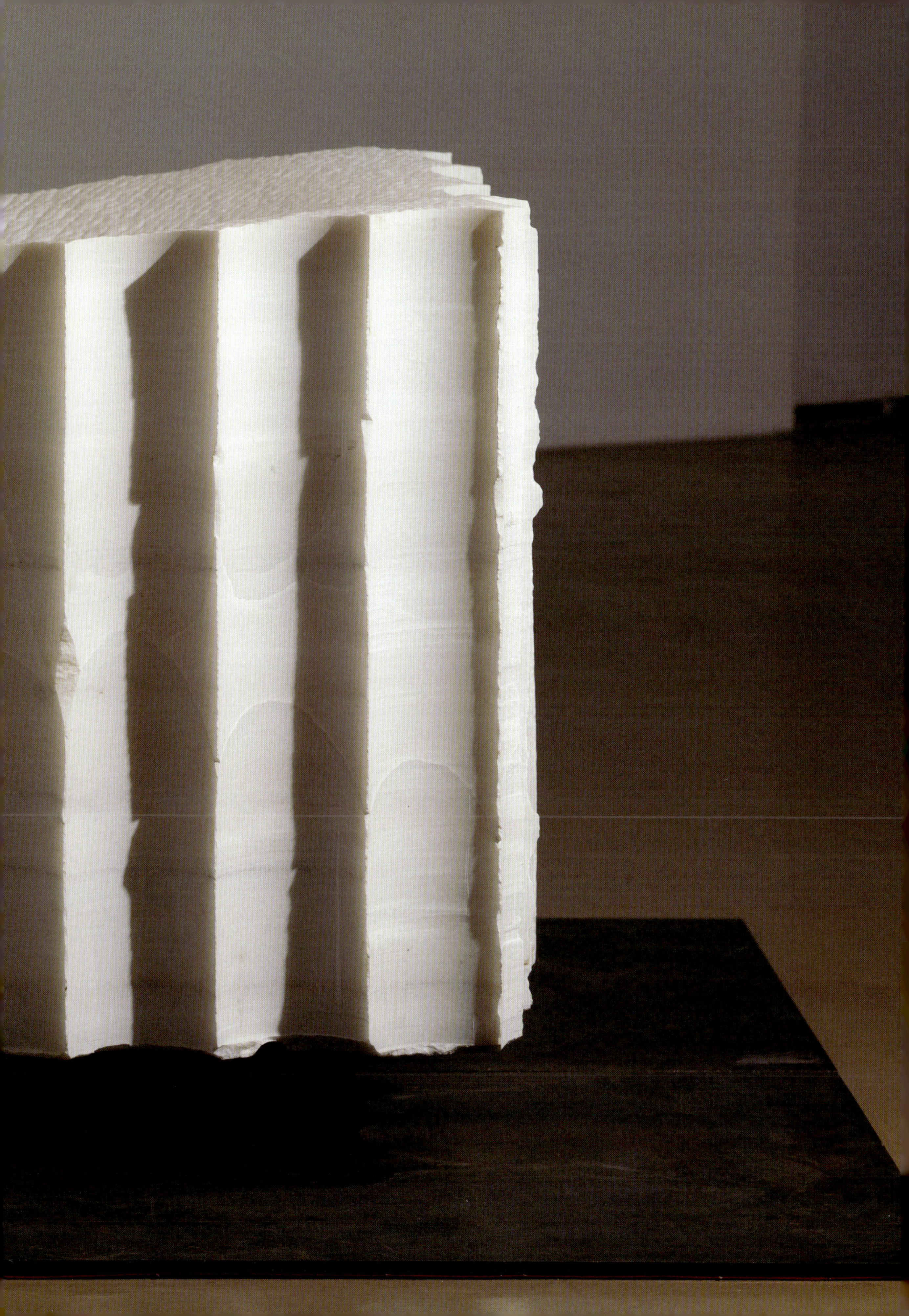

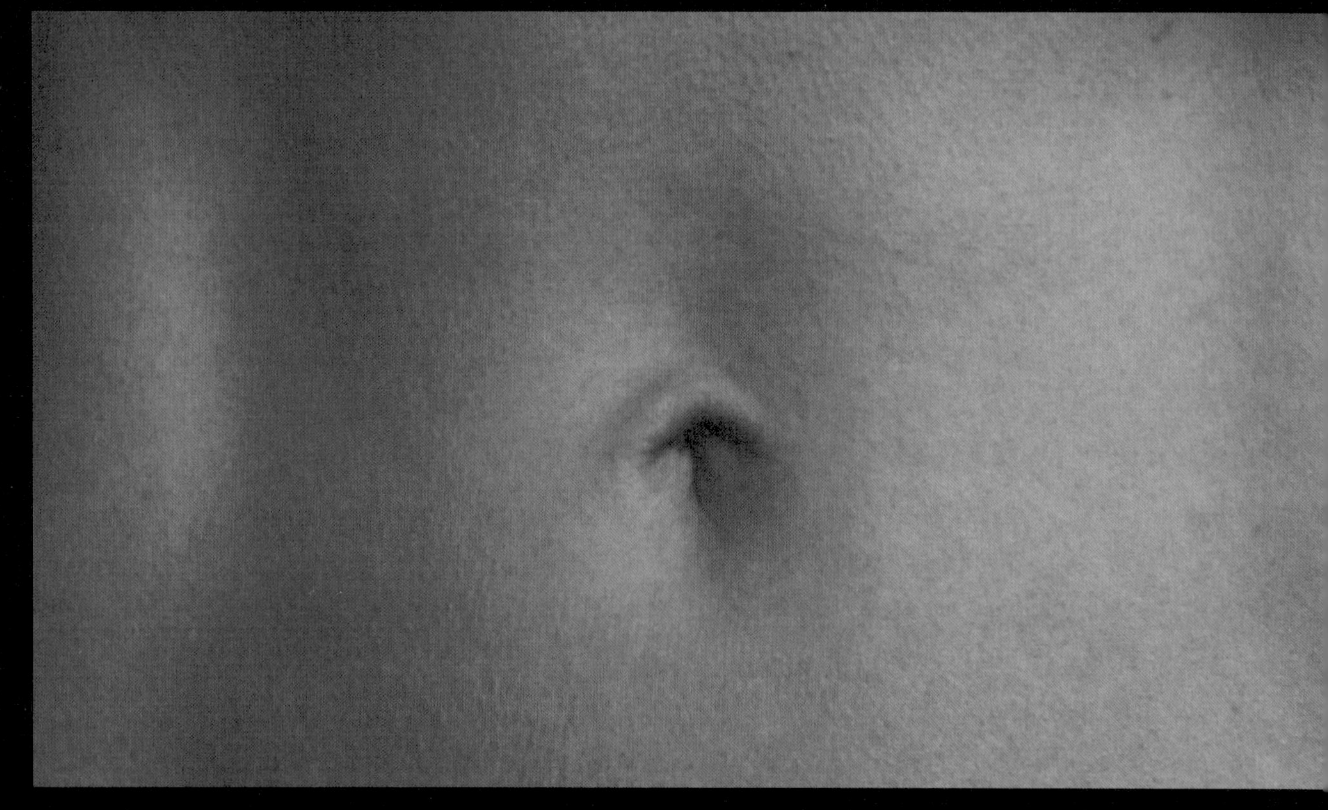

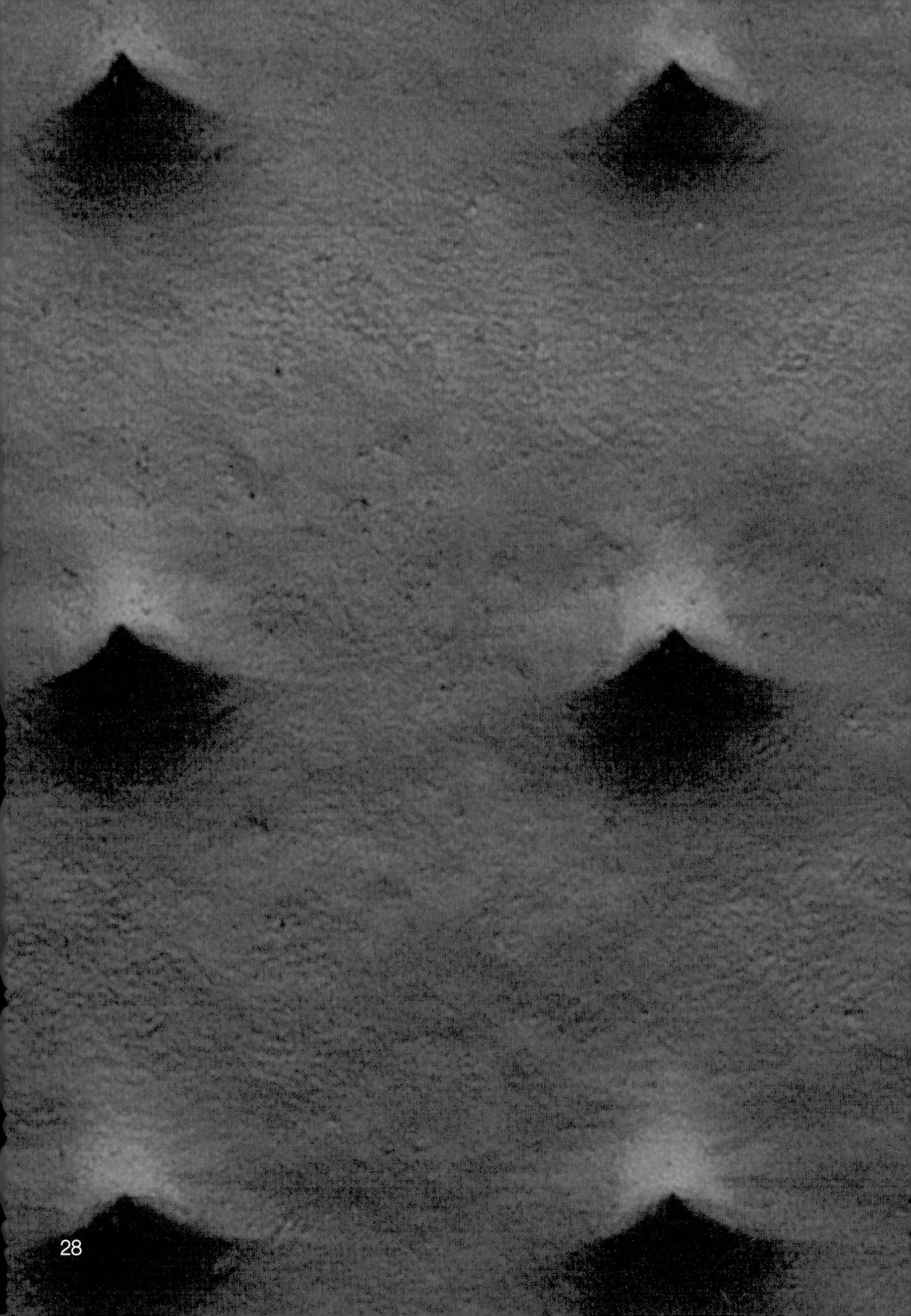

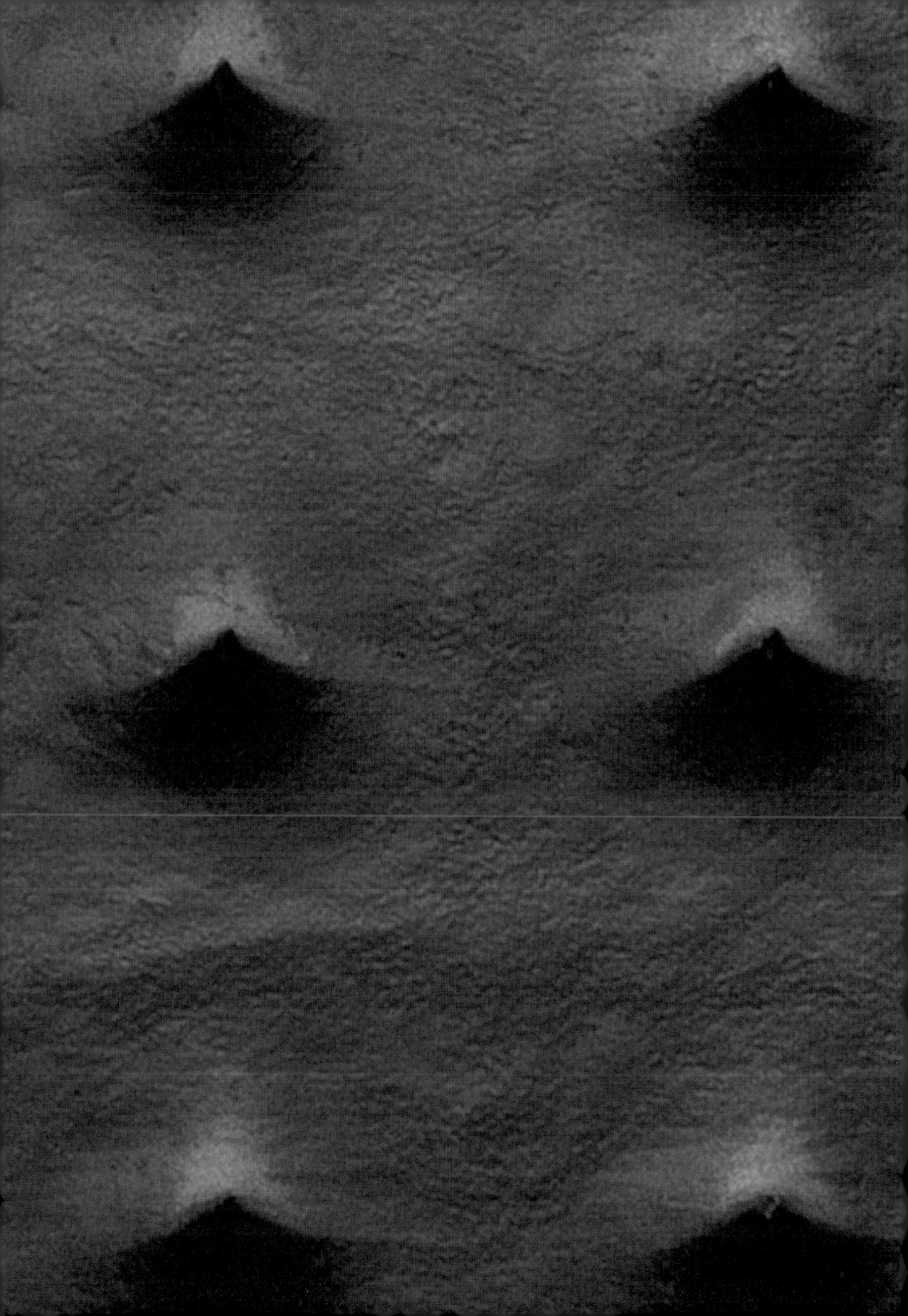

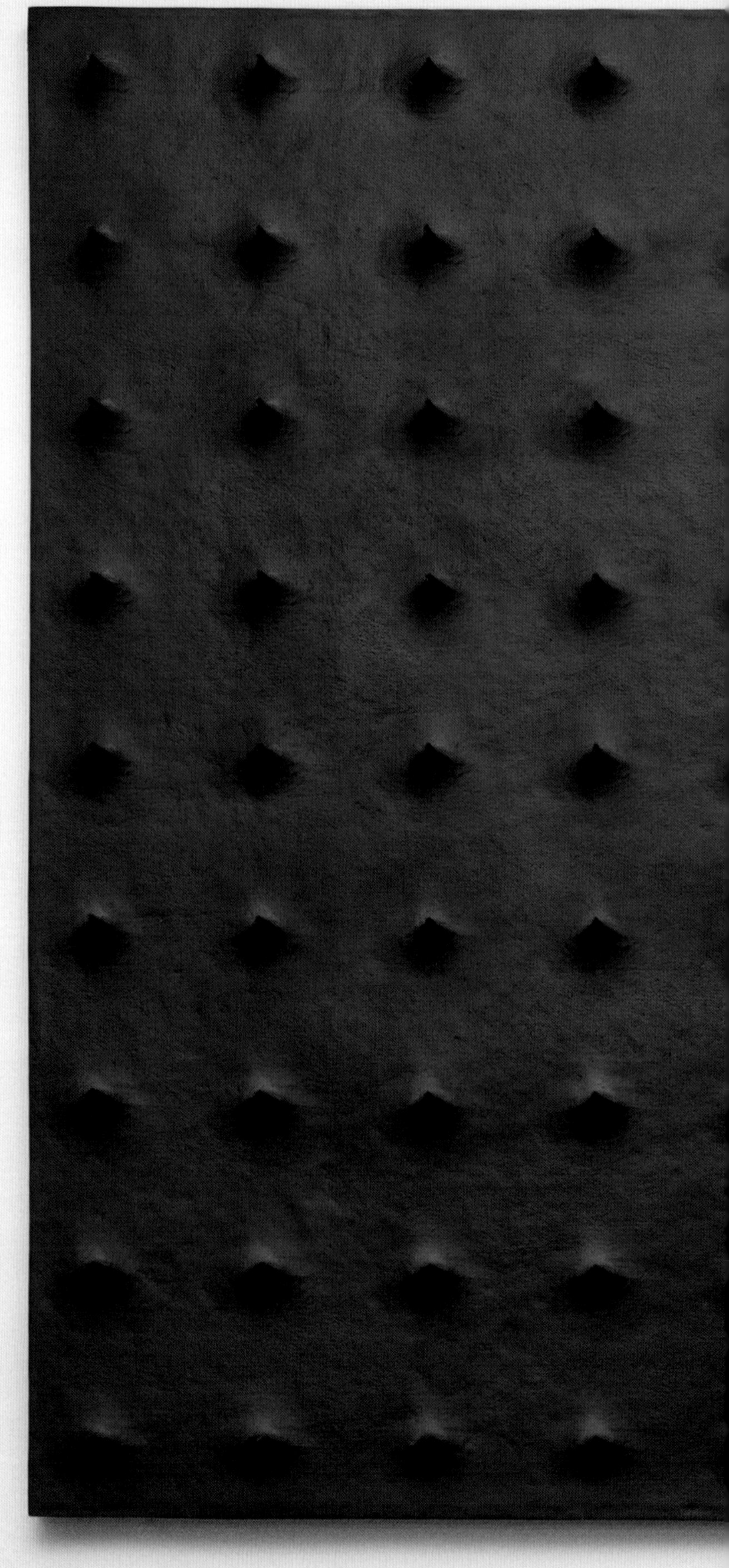

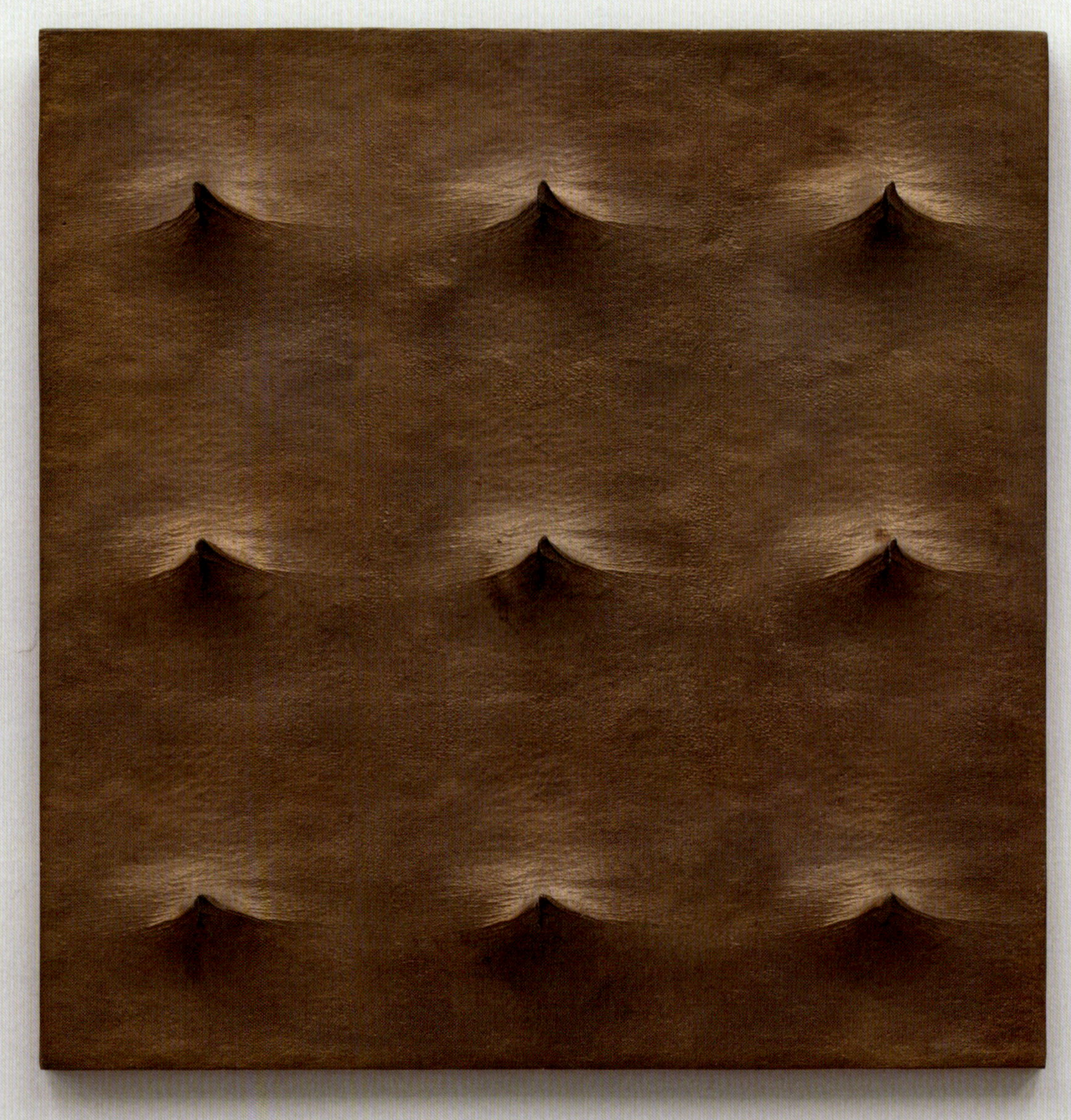

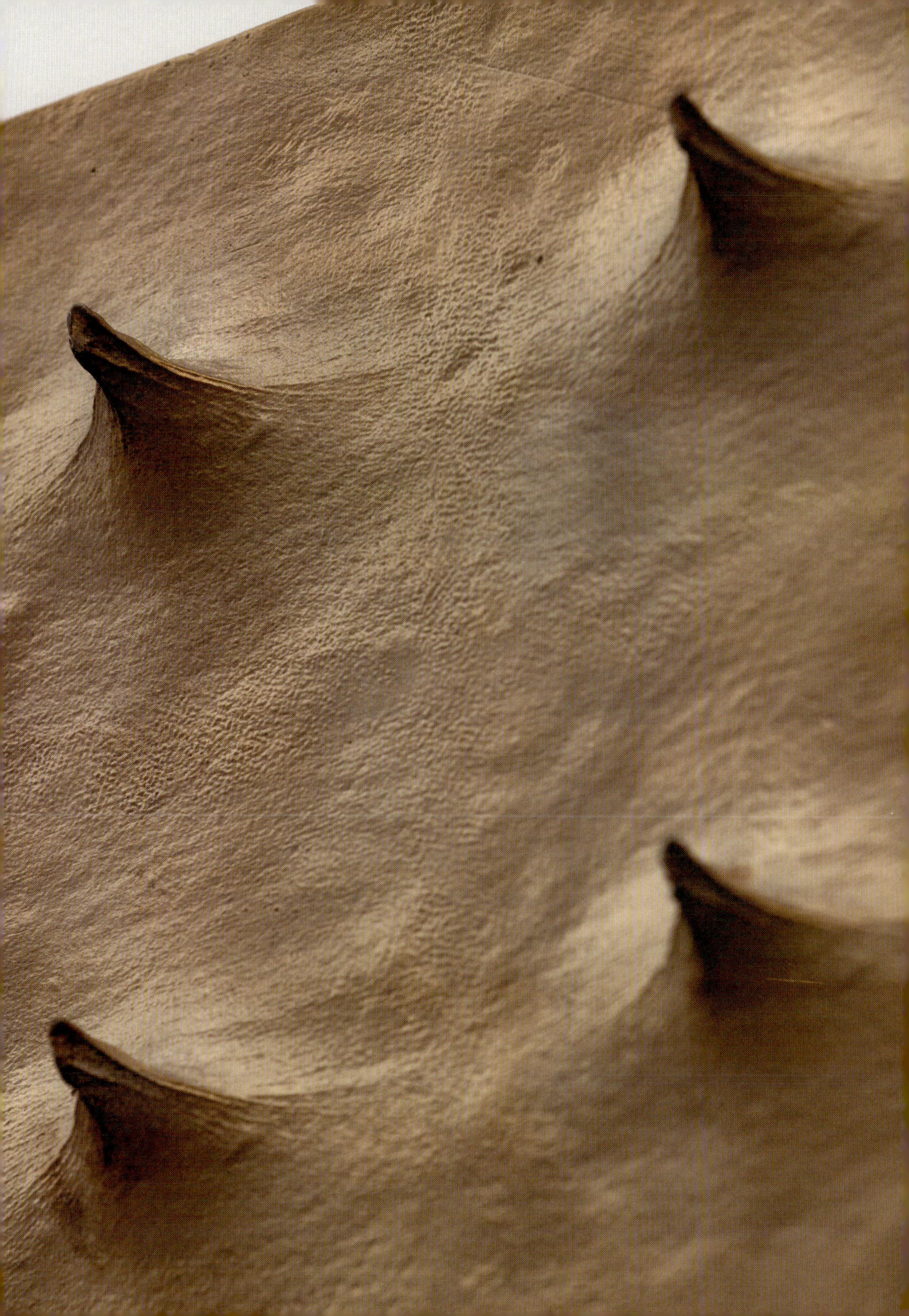

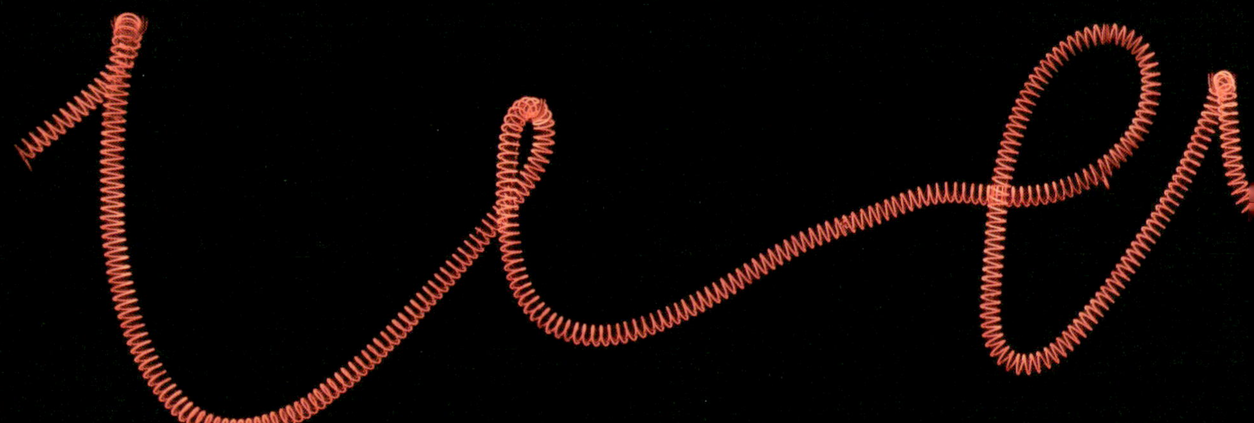

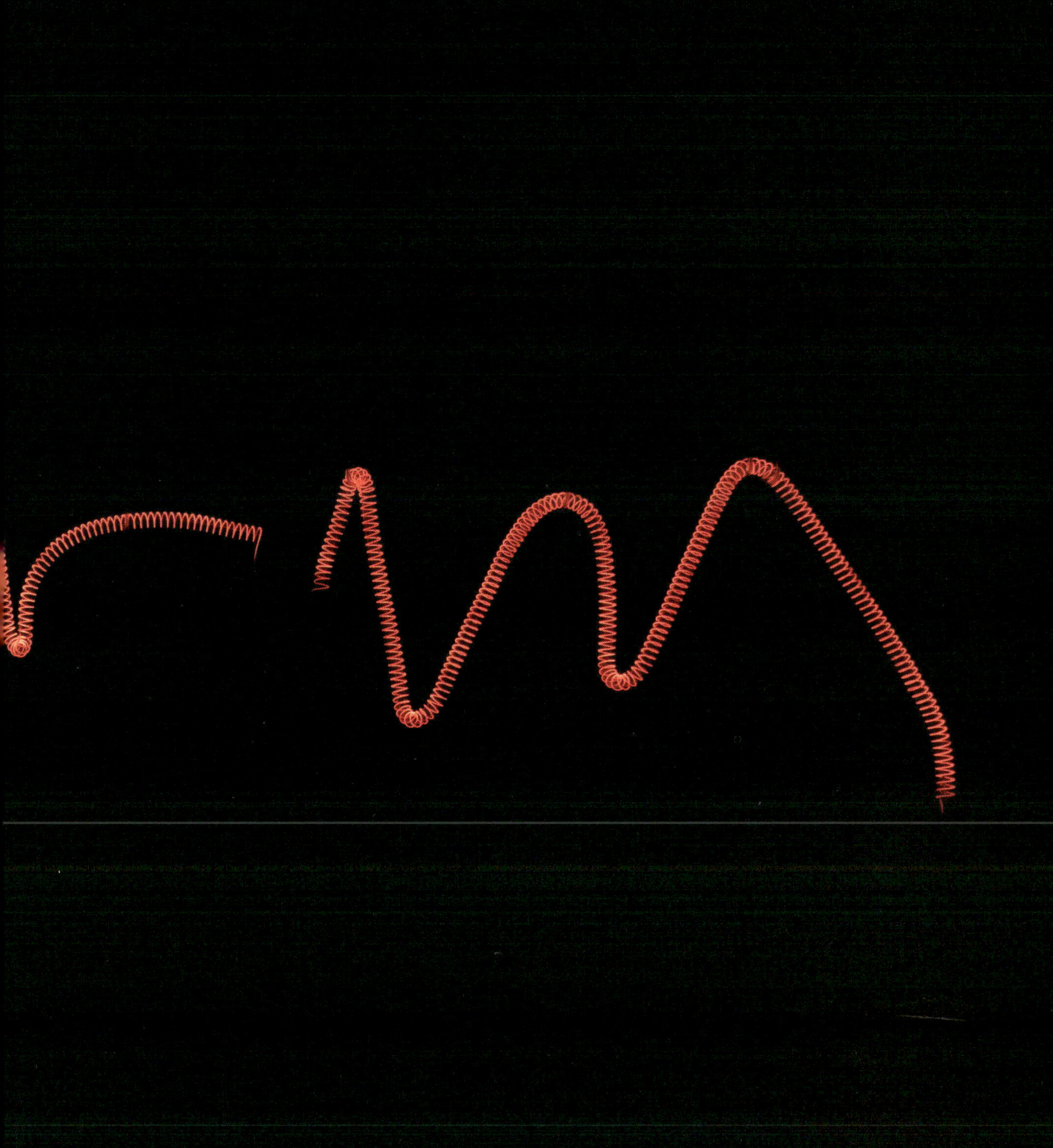

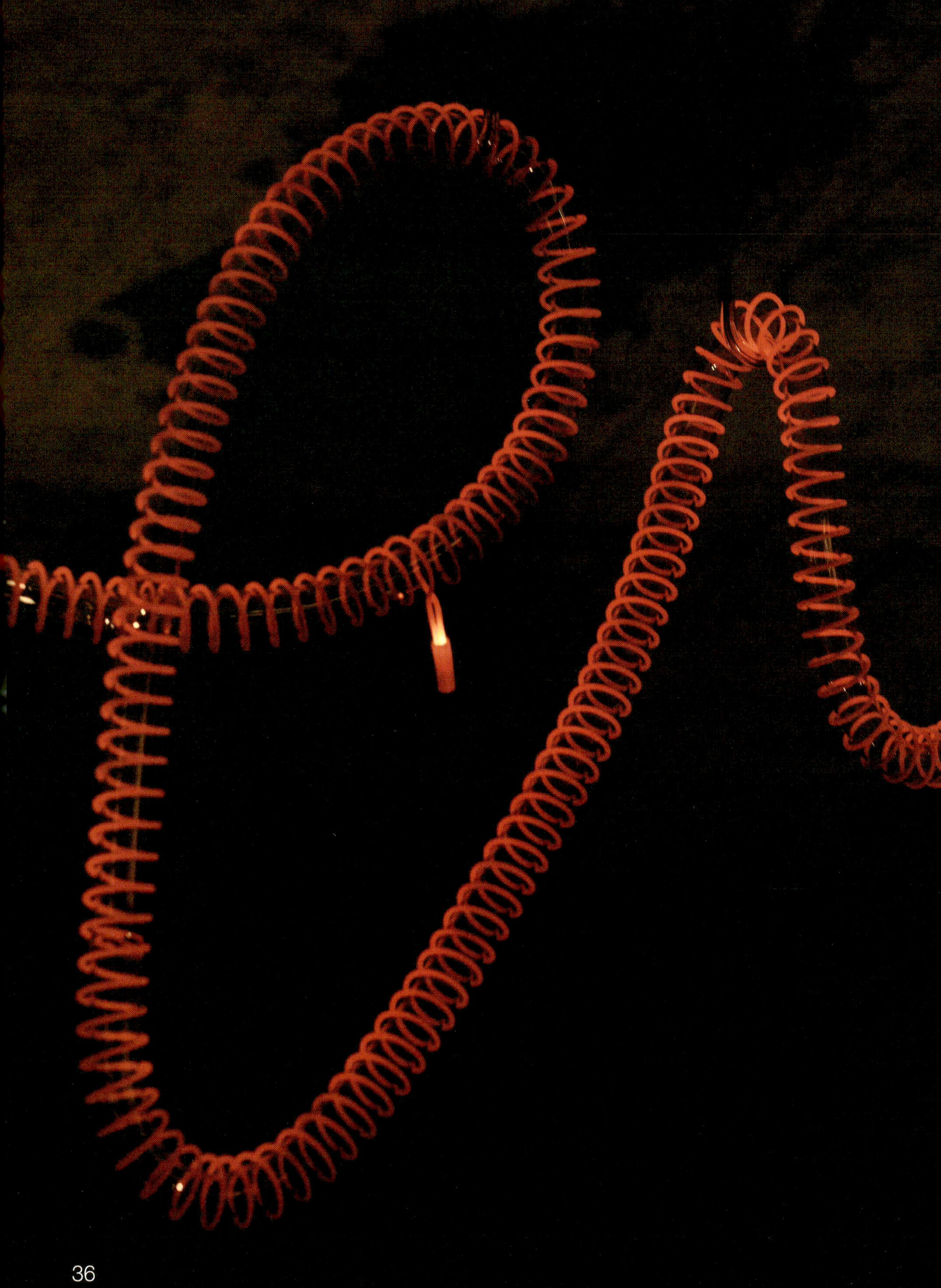

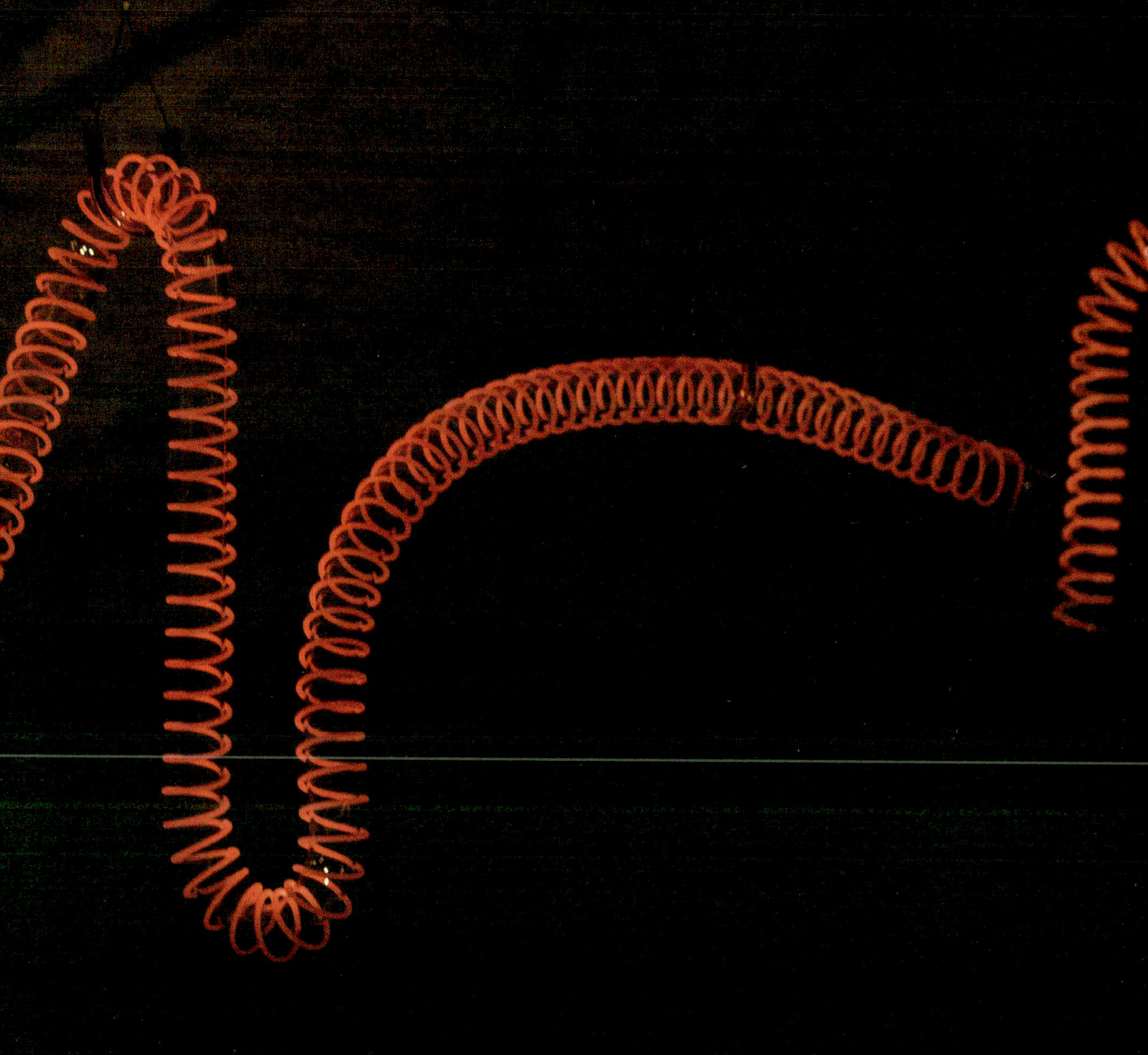

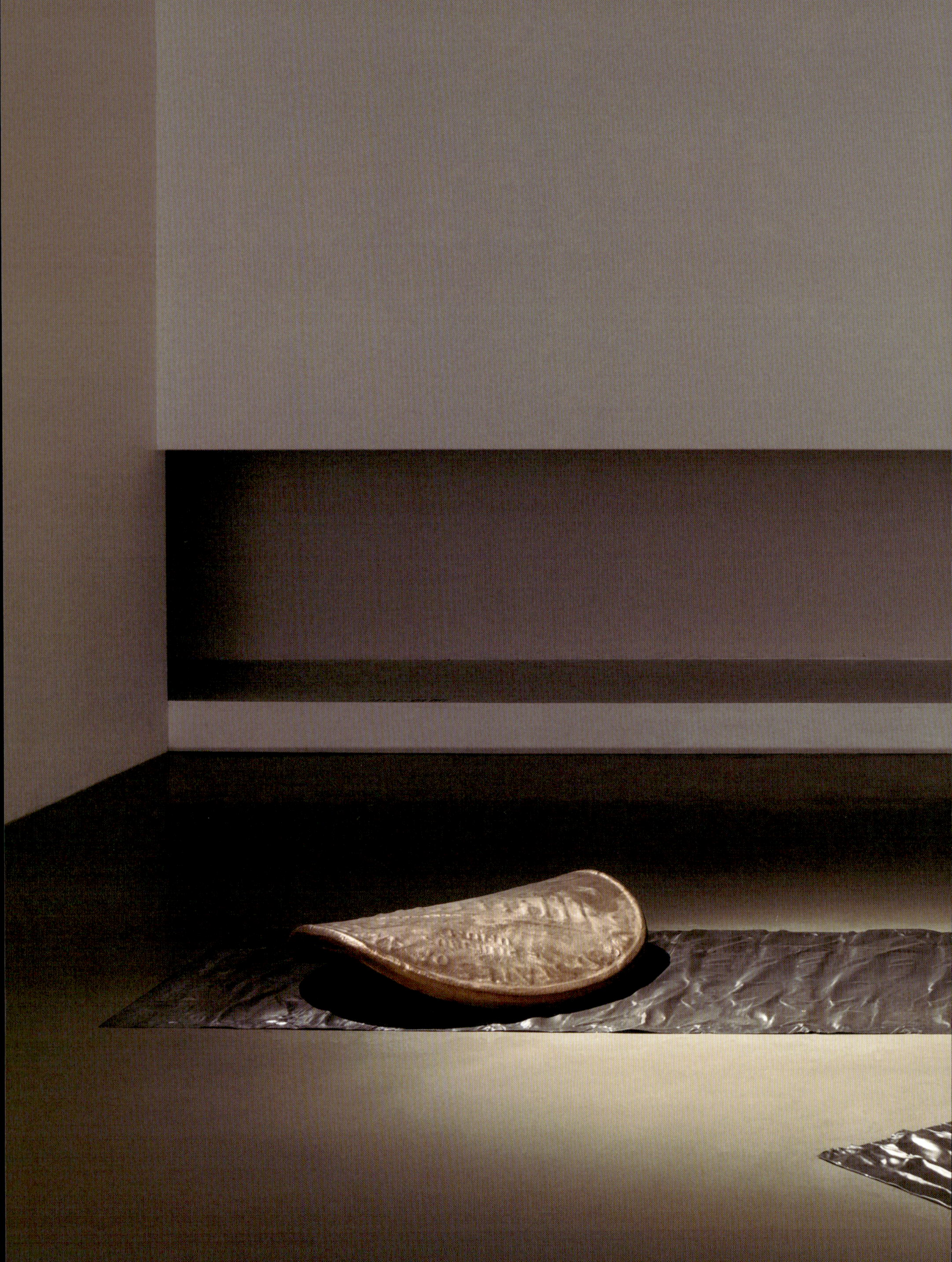

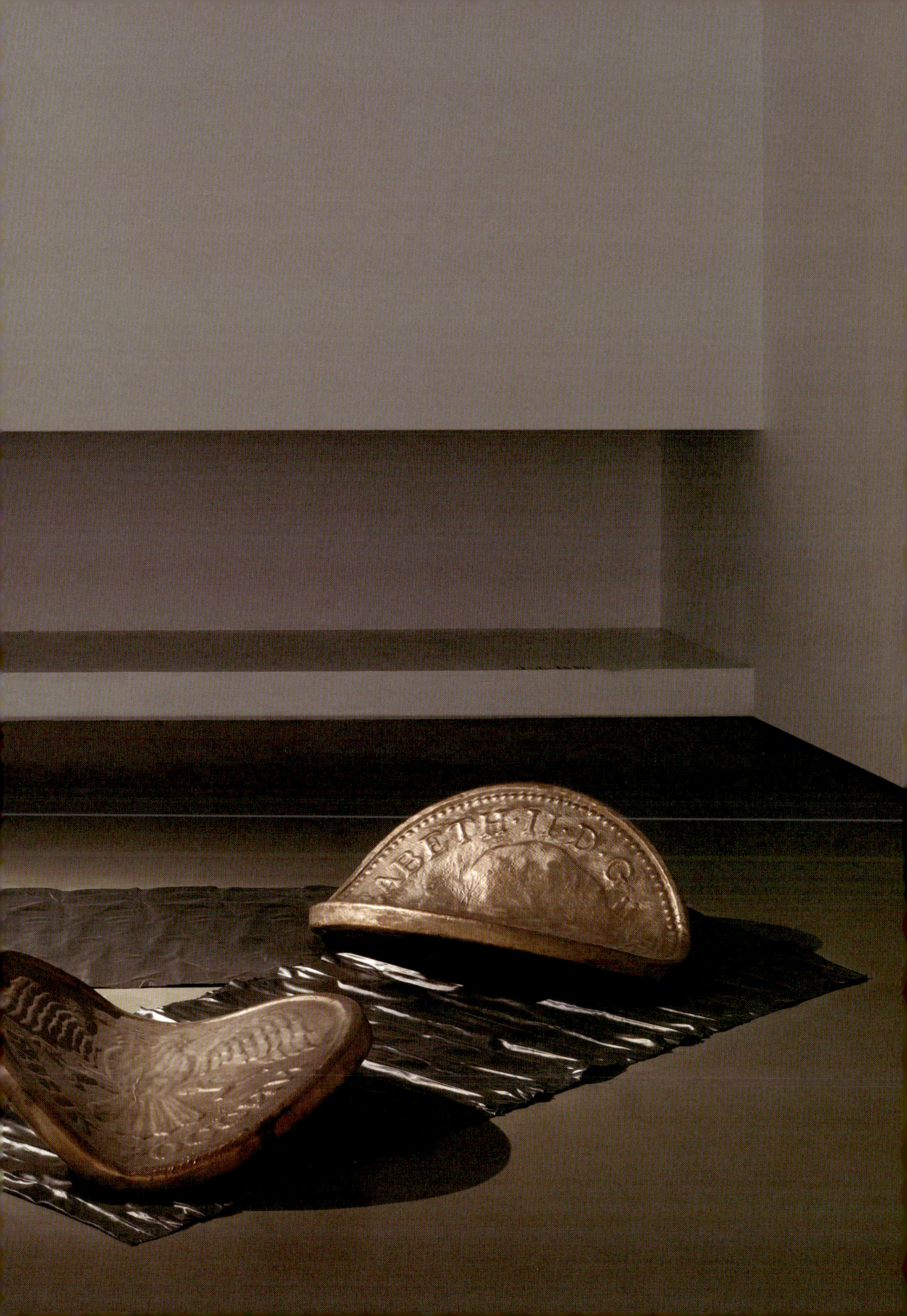

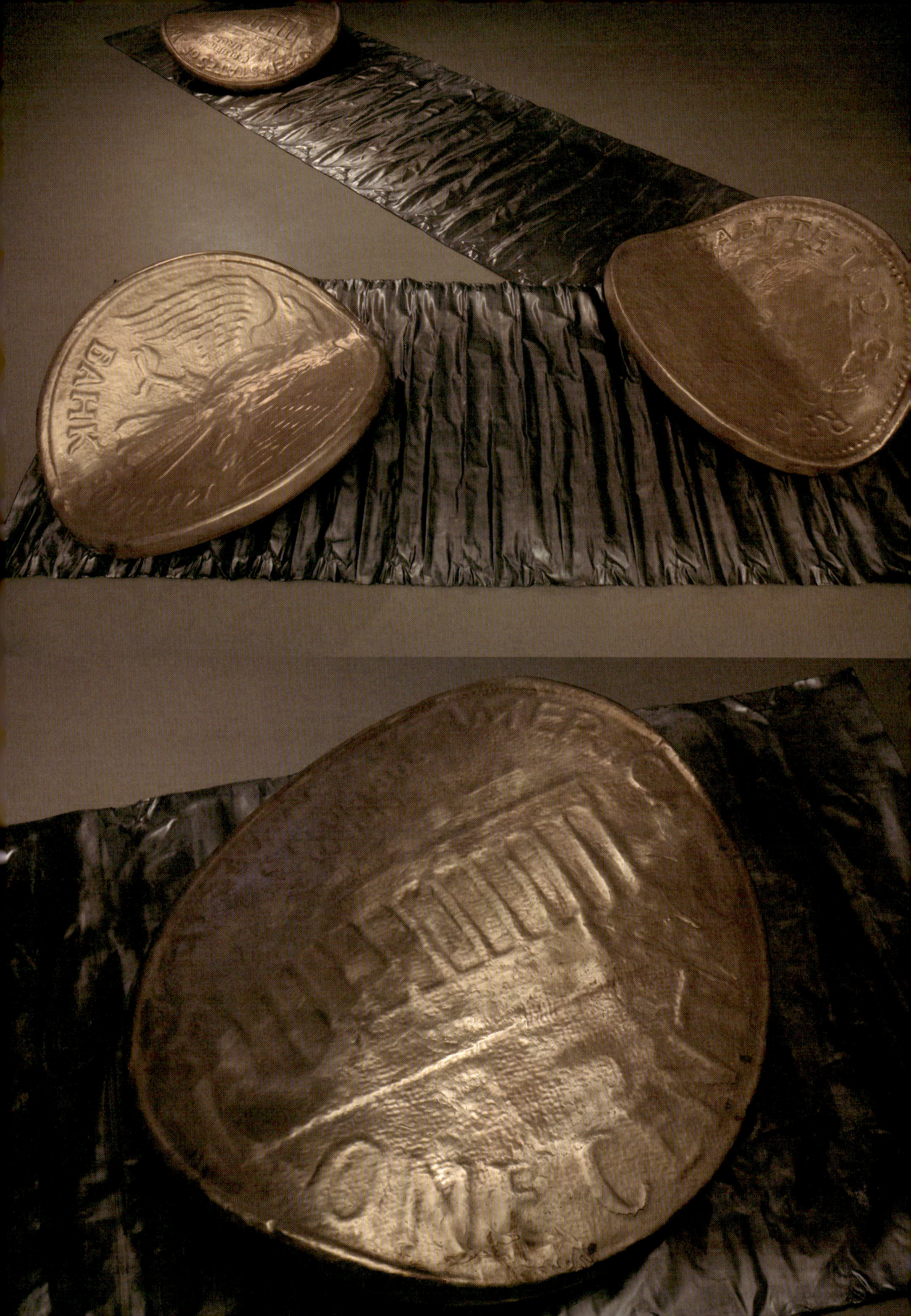

恩睦哲

阅读李怒

综述

在中国新冠疫情封控最激烈的最后几个月，亦是俄乌战争和世界经济下行的正当时，李怒在今日美术馆举办了他的首个机构个展。面对中国乃至全球社会的状况和担忧，艺术家提出了新颖的评注，讨论的议题包括个人自由、社会价值观、个体在社会中的角色以及地缘政治的张力等。李怒试图在东西方之间建立联系，不论是在思想还是哲学方面，抑或通过某种特定的材料来提醒我们不同文化间的共通之处。他展示了一系列充满多样性，同时也紧密相连的作品，其中包括观念性的作品，以文本和身体为媒介的雕塑及影像作品。尽管每件作品都独具一格，却都与展览中其他作品有着微妙而昭然的互动，呈现出完整的作品体系。

在进入艺术生涯中期时，多数创作者往往固守一种有辨识度的风格和可预测的范式；再不然则固守他们为人所熟知的特定媒介或材料，从而得以将自己的名字和某些视觉语言绑定在一起。这种可预测性或熟悉感很容易取悦观众——使我们在看到某件新作品的第一眼就能"认出那位艺术家"。李怒的作品拒绝了这种舒适圈；相反，他挑战我们要不断学习他每件作品的新语汇，并重新与之互动。

字，字，字

李怒在意文字。他有意识地对这些内容进行细致选择，上至展览及作品标题，下至他的文字装置。哲学、文学和一些歌词中的概念，轻易便能在他的作品中交汇。李怒目前常驻北京，他这一代观念艺术家受益于东西方两边的艺术教育，他本人在伦敦皇家艺术学院取得雕塑硕士学位——他对吸收欧亚两端的文学、哲学思想，也显得非常娴熟。

他在今日美术馆的展览标题受到阿根廷作家博尔赫斯的启发："没有什么建于磐石，一切皆在流沙之上。但我们的责任就是建造，仿佛流沙就是磐石……"[1]艺术家提醒我们，博尔赫斯这句话与禅宗及中国哲学"一沙一世界"观念的相通性。[2]沙虽说是石头的最小单位，却更能承压。[3]或许，这句诗的重要性就在于，不论个体所处的环境多么动荡、充满不确定性，一旦投身其中，进入社会的每个单元，便能展现犹如磐石的坚韧特质。

在今日美术馆高耸的红砖外墙表面，迎接观众的是一件大型文字装置——《今夕是何年》（若非另有说明，所有提及作品均为2022年创作）。艺术家别出心裁地用英文写道："今天是什么日子？"（WHAT'S THE DATE TODAY?）这组文字以一系列大型不锈钢字母构成，在呼应馆名之外，他用"日期"的概念实则有意提示：即便社会进步停滞，甚至处于倒退之中，时间依然在嘀嗒声中不断流逝。作品关涉到一种纷乱的过往、动荡的当下以及我们向往看到的美好未来。"今夕是何年"原是北宋诗人和书法家苏轼（1037—1101）的《水调歌头》唱词。在这件转换成英文的装置作品中，李怒将原词中的"年"换为"日"，意在回应古时"天上一日，人间一年"的说法；另外，他也将这点与歌词后段的感受联系在一起：即便"人有悲欢离合"，但仍能"千里共婵娟"。借此，李怒也表达了在面对如今发生的种种危机时，愿所有个体依然拥有共情的能力。

同样从歌词中找到文字标题的，还包括李怒另一件装置作品《灵在水上》，这件作品陈列在今日美术馆展厅橱窗中。作品标题源自美国著名歌手、作曲家鲍勃·迪伦所作的一首情歌——而歌曲本身则引用了圣经《创世记》中的一节经文。明黄色的背景墙上立着四把椅子，椅脚都固定在墙上，我们看到座位有明显烧焦的痕迹。地面上散落着八个旧的玻璃渔获浮球。作品让我们想起那些已经搁置太久或从未实现的旅行计划，还有不再流动的人群。

另一类运用文本的装置作品亦能体现艺术家将语言作为艺术表达形式的兴趣。在作品《但愿上天让人理解并感受到自己的和他人的愿望》中，镍铬丝拼写出"温暖"（warm）一词，在黑暗的房间里断断续续发出热烈的红光。在"warm"最后一个字母之前有个空隙，读起来也因此像是"war"，战争——尽管我们期望着有着宜人暖意的"温暖"，但"战争"却是灼热的，以至于灼伤我们的皮肤。事实上，在展览现场，如果靠这件作品更近，我们的皮肤确实会被烧伤，只不过李怒造了半截墙隔开高温。即便如此，除了作品实际的热度之外，我们也感受到目前持续不断的局部战争所引发的苦难——亦在沉痛燃烧着，这些战争导致大量的恐怖活动，在不同程度上给我们所有人带来伤痛。

作品《羊脂球》是个填充羊脂的立方体装置，从中也能相应地找到他对西方文学的引用。标题源于法国作家莫泊桑的同名中篇小说，其中一位"卖弄风骚"的妓女角色，因为身材"娇小、圆润、丰满"，人们称她为羊脂球。[4]事实上，在这群乘坐马车逃离战争的乘客中，要算是她最值得尊敬了。她不仅分享自己带来的所有存粮，并且当这些人被扣为人质时，她做出了最终的牺牲：这个羊脂球应允满足敌军士兵的生理需求。在她做出牺牲后，所有人都回到了马车上，却没有人感激羊脂球，甚至也没有人给她任何食物。莫泊桑写道，他们"先牺牲了她，然后拒绝了她"。[5]如果说，在李怒的视觉语言中，羊脂代表人，那么，它应该是大量工人和企业的象征，在疫情大流行期间，一旦这些服务不再被需要，就立刻遭到丢弃。

李怒仰慕萨特的文笔，这从楼上展厅有几件受到这位法国哲人作家启发的作品中不难发现。例如，声音装置作品《苍蝇》便是受到萨特1943年的话剧《苍蝇》的启发。[6]这件装置作品让我们进到黑房间，耳边环绕着苍蝇的嗡嗡声。在另一件名为《为什么不能让天使和恶魔都亲吻我》的油画中，同一主题进行了视觉上的延续，画面中，两只大苍蝇背对背，身体和翅膀触碰在一起。作品标题或许也在暗示善恶、对错之间的差别并不那么容易界定。一般来说，苍蝇并不受人们待见，然而，就如在古埃及，苍蝇却备受尊敬。[7]

在《为什么不能让天使和恶魔都亲吻我》对面摆着一件青铜雕塑作品《命名是一种悲伤的行为》，双联幅的结构似乎在模仿对面画作中的两只苍蝇。这件青铜雕塑的英文标题"神与国王都有痛苦的秘密"（The Painful Secret of Gods and Kings）出自萨特《苍蝇》的台词，其寓意则延伸到雕塑的背面：一块石头被分成两半，两个截面上都刻着大写英文字母的"自由"（LIBERTY）一词；一面是单词的正序书写，另一面则是反向书写。最后，白色大理石装置《死亡是唯一的出口》是对萨特1944年热门戏剧《禁闭》的致敬——戏剧围绕三个受困地狱的灵魂之间的焦灼关系而展开。作品由一个小巧的乳白色大理石盒子构成，大理石表面有穿过的孔洞，倒置阅读则是代表"出口"的盲文。盒子上方嵌入两只小小的金色苍蝇。如果有人靠得很近，便会听到作品发出电击的声音。唯有当观众稍许改变观看这件作品的位置时，才能看到在背后镜子的反射之下，盲文词"出口"的正序书写。这件作品正如中文标题《死亡是唯一的出口》的字面意涵。

李怒作品中另一个反复出现的特质则是对双关语的使用。作品《硬陛》的英文标题"我们信仰黄金"（In Gold We Trust）借用了一句出现在美元货币上的美式表达——"我们信仰上帝"（In God We Trust）。这组由三件大型青铜雕塑组成的作品，呈扭曲的硬币形状，被放大至一种神话般的比例。据艺术家所说，这个作品还受到了英国小说家毛姆1919年出版的小说《月亮与六便士》的启发。毛姆在这本小说中检视了"人们在抬头看月亮的时候，常常便会忘记脚下的六便士"这种说法。对于毛姆而言，月亮是能够代表艺术和美的理想领域，而六便士则代表了现实世界和人际关系。[8]李怒将这句引言与佛教文本联系起来——亦是一种桥接东西方文化的方式。在佛教经典中，月亮象征着真理，而手指仅是指向真理的工具。[9]正如《楞伽经》所说："如愚见指月，观指不观月，计著文字者，不见我真实。"[10]

有意思的是，艺术家随机选择了三种货币，把最小面额放大，并抹去货币自身大部分容易被识别的标记。比如那件以美元硬币为原型的货币雕塑，李怒用"Gold"（黄金）取代了"God"（上帝）。"我们

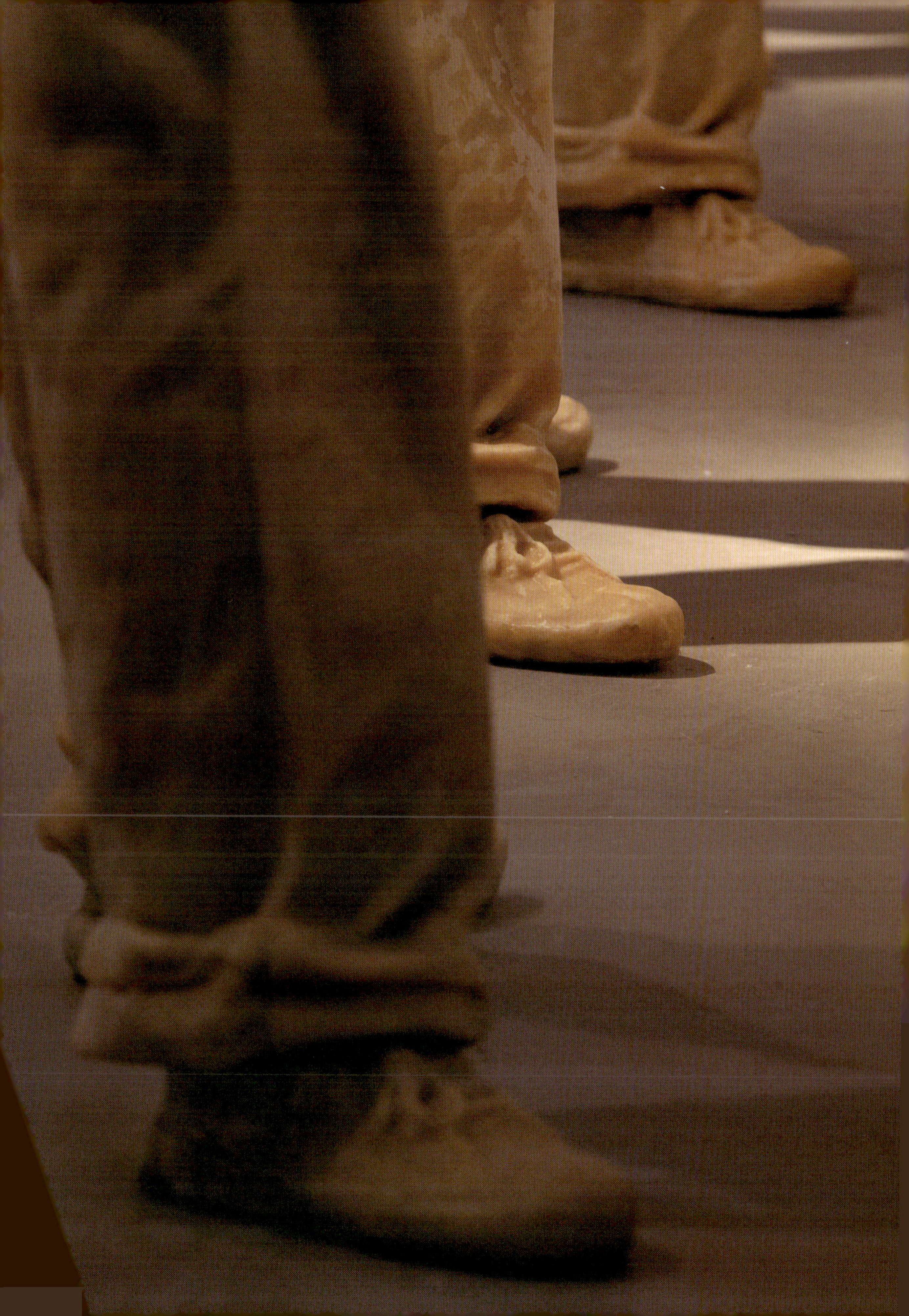

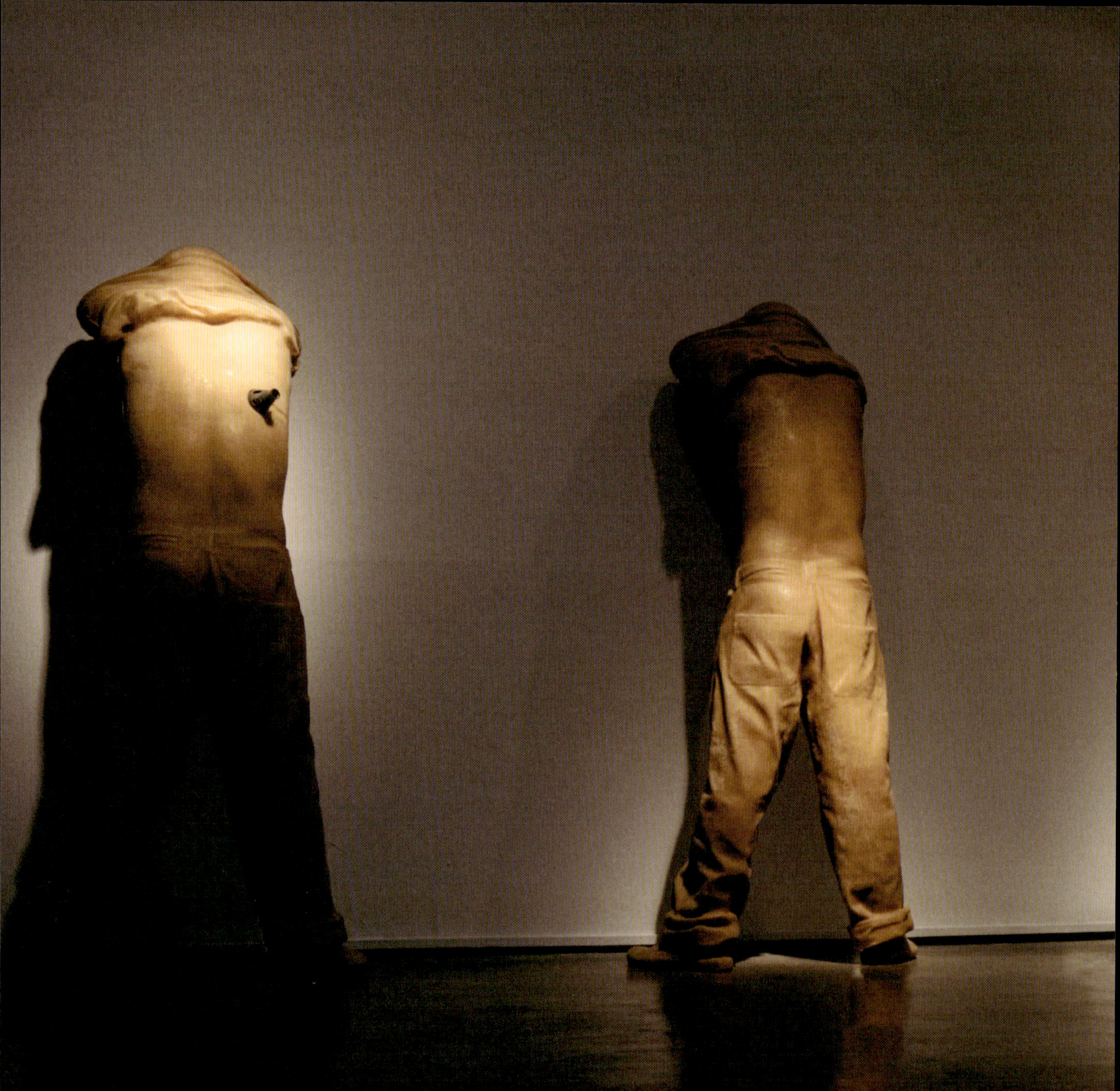

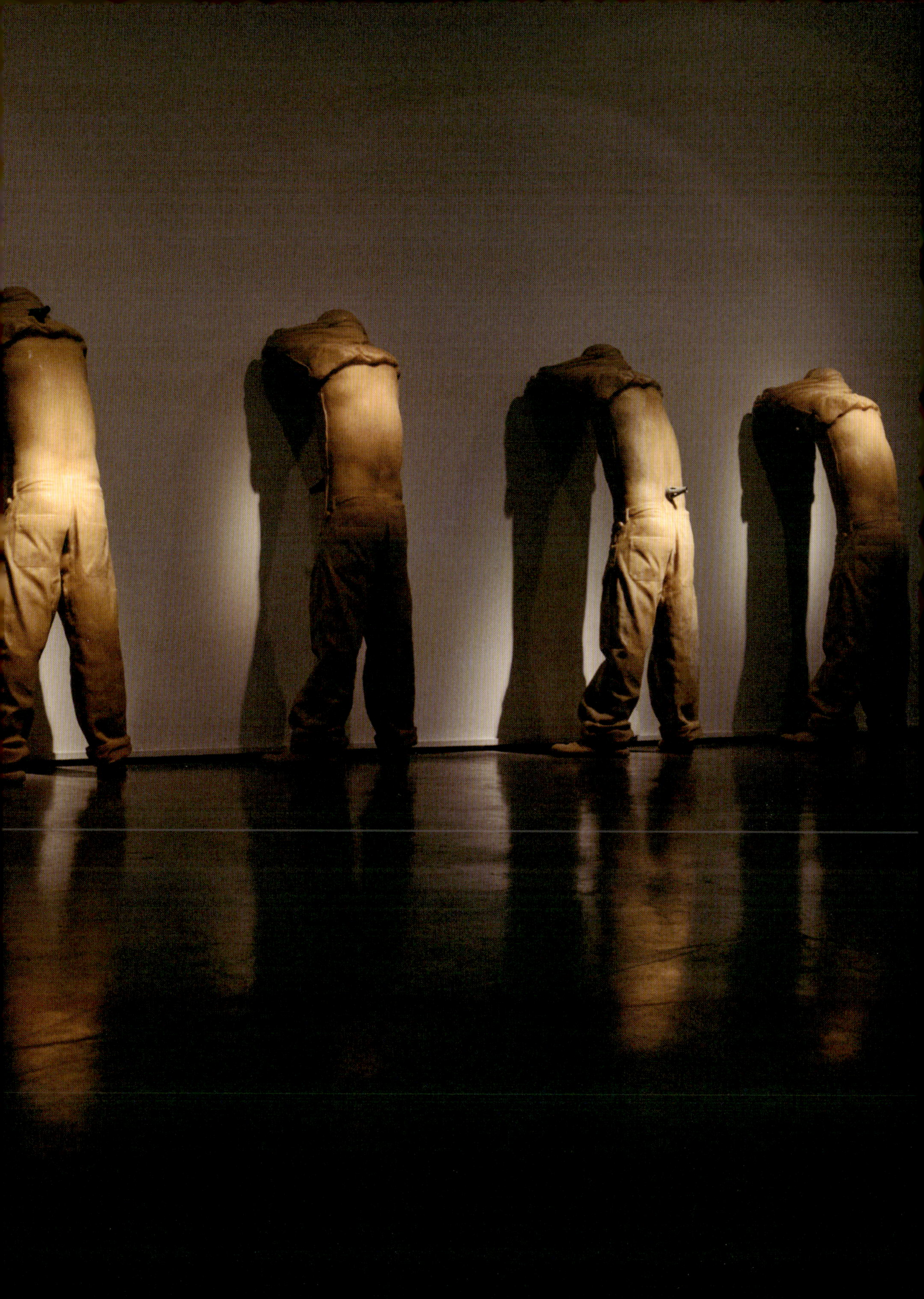

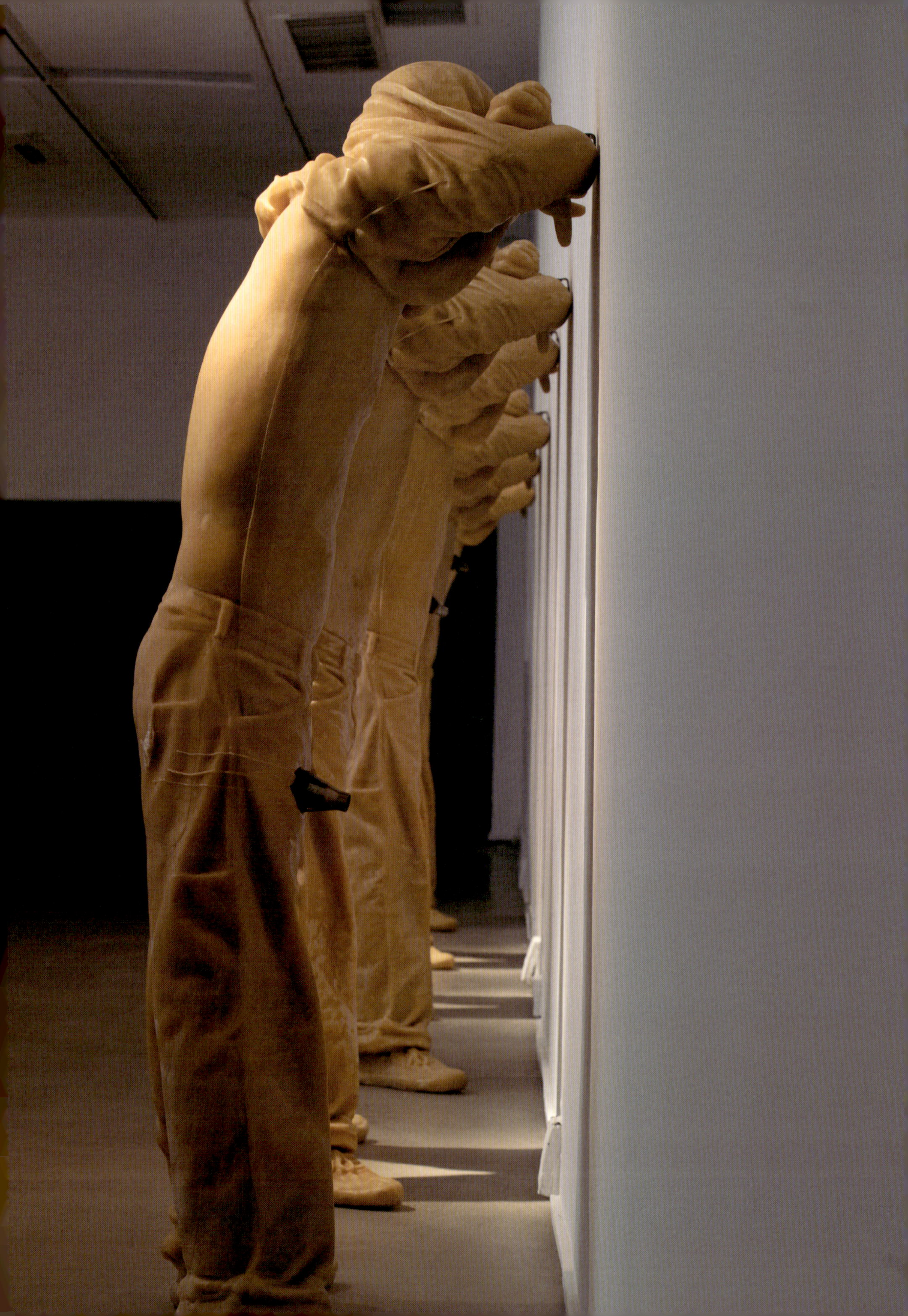

信仰黄金"这句话提出了一个问题：当我们不再仰赖神或是某种至高无上的存在时，社会将发生什么变化？李怒实际上是在暗示我们的价值观是通过物质文化表现出来的。在一个不重视至善或神圣力量的社会中，金钱、劳动力和人便会被视为仅仅是可供交易的对象——这也是萨特戏剧中所描绘的地狱场景。

媒介＋材料＝信息

在任何艺术作品中，选取不同媒材作为信息的传递都是至关重要的。李怒的所有作品——从羊脂、蜂蜡和水银这些非传统材料，到包括大理石和青铜在内的更为传统的材料——在材料选择范围的广度上令人瞩目。尽管他受到的是雕塑训练，但在媒介的选取上，却远远超出传统雕塑的范畴：这次展览中有基于文本的作品，有声音装置、视频和绘画作品，似乎比起单一媒介，选用复杂多样的媒材更能表达我们所处的世界。

李怒的创作在材料选取方面表现出了一种特别的观照。举个例子，在创作《未竟之柱》的过程中，艺术家在找到合适的媒介之前比较过四种不同石材。他最后选择了抛光后的汉白玉，将其打造成十一边形的柱体。汉白玉的名称本身就有精致和光亮的意涵。然而，他却按照纽约自由女神像的底座——即伍德堡的形状进行雕琢，不无讽刺意味的是，此处曾用为军事堡垒。在石头内部，李怒放置了一根直径10厘米的铝柱。雕塑柱体顶着一块装饰圆盘，中心则有一颗水银玻璃球。如果玻璃破裂，水银流出与铝柱融合，将发生絮凝现象：大块絮状物开始增生，乱糟糟地形成块团，看起来也是对自由女神像一种简约版的再现。

选择水银作为材料并不寻常，除了众多象征联想外，也进一步突显这件雕塑的不同之处。水银的一个独特性在于，它是唯一在室温下呈液态的金属。它亦毒亦药（汞蒸气有剧毒）。此外，它还是一个与东西方社会都有联系的元素。在中国，它被视为道家炼就长生不老药的原材料。在广泛研究后，专家认为秦始皇陵中就有大量汞元素的遗留。它有多种用途：保存尸体，作为防腐蚀的药剂，也防止盗窃。[11]或许，李怒就是喜欢某种具有双重意涵的矛盾之处：到底，汞是能够建设大厦，还是让它颓倾？

对于水银的使用也串联起展览中的另一件作品——将温度计一字排开的小型装置《温度计》。温度计是亲民平等的：家家户户都有，被依赖也被信赖。不过，在新冠病毒流行期间，温度计却成了限制自由的工具："异常"的检测结果会让民众无法进入超市、乘坐公共交通或是去上学、工作。而李怒的温度计则让水银不再是提供温度的读数，而是根据"自由的度量"而上升：温度刻度也随之被这些词替代。

正如我们在讨论《羊脂球》这件作品时所提到的，同样在李怒作品中扮演重要角色的另一种非常规媒介便是羊脂。艺术家从2019年开始使用这种材料，当时他在为中蒙边境的巨型场地特定装置《铁幕》进行制作。他先是铸了模型，注入水，随后冻成超过2米高、近1米宽、长达36米的巨型冰墙。当铸模开始渗漏时，当地牧民建议艺术家用羊脂填充结构中的缝隙。这个方法奏效了。于是在2021年，李怒于马刺画廊的个展"一片和平"中，他在作品《G弦上的咏叹调》中以较小尺幅铸造了一堵用羊脂填补的墙。即便如此，总共也用到了约16吨的羊脂。在作品《羊脂球》中，艺术家收集了那些已经倒闭的企业的印章。这些小小的印章刻字从羊脂的堆积中凸显出来，正如李怒所言，它们"在脂体的表面形成伤口般的结痂状"。[12]疫情期间，这些企业在动荡的经济漩涡中被吞噬，严重影响到人们的生计。每个公司印章都代表了一家功败垂成的企业，这反过来又影响到数以百计、甚至更多的人，仿如被堆积的脂肪所包围。

还有一种李怒使用的罕见媒介则是蜂蜡。在今日美术馆的展览中，六尊真人大小的雕塑作品便以此为媒介。这组名为《瀑布》的作品，每个人物都以艺术家自己的身体为模型。他们的姿势透露出一种脆弱感：靠在墙上，双臂折叠环抱着头，背朝观众露出柔软的背部身体。蜂蜡有很强的延展性——它容易变形、融化——进一步强化了这些形象的脆弱性。这也和《但愿上天让人理解并感受到自己的和他人的愿望》、《未竟之柱》和《温度计》这些涉及"身 体"、"热"和"温度"的作品有深切的关联。

李怒对于非常规材料的使用也延展到了日常生活当中。在《如果你看到她，问她好》（标题同样来自鲍勃·迪伦的歌词），艺术家用两件胶布连帽雨衣，一大一小，面对着悬挂，似乎在暗示着亲密的对话，或是私下会面——观众有自己的解读。从形式上来说，这件装置是前文提到的《为什么不能让天使和恶魔都亲吻我》的反转——两只苍蝇的身影面向相反方向，身体与翅膀相触着。

这些丰富多样的材料让李怒将不同的作品凝结在一起，形成具有统一性的创作体系；在各种话题的信息传递上产生回响。

身体，我，我们

对于任何艺术家来说，他们的身体本身便是最容易接触到的媒介。李怒将自己的身体作为许多作品——包括持续性表演、视频和雕塑的出发点。他对肉身的运用并不是仅仅出于便利，而是出于观众能够有熟悉且能理解的共同经验，从而打下共情的基础。与其说他是在强调自我，不如说他是在呼吁一种共通的人性、共同的理解。

如前所述，六件真人尺寸的雕塑《瀑布》以艺术家自己的身体为模具创作而成。通过蜡这种软性媒介和身体姿态的脆弱感，作品能引发观众的共鸣。值得注意的是，六件雕塑分别有一个喷枪的管嘴突出于身体的某个部位，这既示意了雕塑的制作过程，也暗示了人作为一个物种的繁衍。

肚脐这个主题——代表了出生印记——则能在一系列名为《世界》的作品中找到。位处这系列作品中心位置的，是一大块汉白玉，其造型则根据艺术家自己的肚脐翻模放大雕刻而来。肚脐朝上，也暗示了一个平躺的身体。李怒做这件雕塑的方式，有点像是古罗马人挖洞作为天上和地下神灵之间的联通。仰卧姿态也提示我们，我们通常以站姿观看世界的角度与躺下时是不同的。[13]

在这件雕塑附近，是一件双屏幕的影像作品：时而是两个肚脐的并置，随着模特缓慢地前后移动，有时只能见到肚脐与后背的并置。对李怒来说，这象征着"人与世界的原初关联"。[14]最后一组作品中，艺术家则用肚脐的负型，它们如尖钩一样，从两块平面铜板上刺出。在英语中，"肚脐凝视"（navel gazing）一词指的是对自我的过分关注：将自己和自己的关切视为宇宙的中心。实际上，李怒所做的恰恰相反：他呈现了一个普世的象征，生命的起源，这是所有人类共同拥有并能够认同的东西。

不论是提示仰卧姿态的汉白玉雕塑，还是用肚脐的负型进行铸模，肚脐在这批雕塑作品中的位置都指向了用一种全新的视角来看待事物。对于李怒而言，这些铜雕"是去中心化的、也是中心多元化的象征"。[15]艺术家提示我们，多元中心或是多种起源应有同时存在的讨论空间：每个国家都应有权以它自身作为中心。

在这些作品中，李怒不仅仅是在用自己的身体进行创作，甚至也调动了观众的身体——他们必须以非常规的方式在展览中穿行，并体验到对身体感官的强烈冲击。展厅中有两面悬挂的墙，观众必须要弯腰从下面通过，才能进入下一个空间。这种对空间的干预也诱发观众的期待，艺术家解释道，这种调度是"先抑后扬"。[16]在展览入口，我们通过第一堵悬挂墙来到作品《未竟之柱》。墙的下缘，艺术家留下一句话："眉毛是你的羽毛吗？"用以论述眉毛是我们身体上最有表现力的特征——尤其是当我们戴起口罩的时候。[17]第二堵悬挂墙则阻挡我们直接近距离观看文字装置作品《但愿上天让人理解并感受到自己的和他人的愿望》。当我们进入展厅空间，站在这堵半墙面前，不仅仅视觉被作品吸引，还有触觉——让我们感受到皮肤的灼烧感。

另一个空间干预行为在楼上展厅的作品《庇护所》中得以窥见。这件由四个部分组成的装置作品中，钢结构的网状隔断墙将空间分为四个截然不同的区域，迫使观众需要按照艺术家设定的顺序从一个空间移动到另一个空间，而移动的顺序对于李怒而言代表了一个人的心态变化。[18]

接着，我们的听觉感知会受到大型装置作品《一切坚固的东西都烟消云散了》（2019）的冲击。当观众踏在这片巨大的的钢板平台时，突然听到震耳欲聋的枪声——当下便被害怕、恐慌和关切他人安

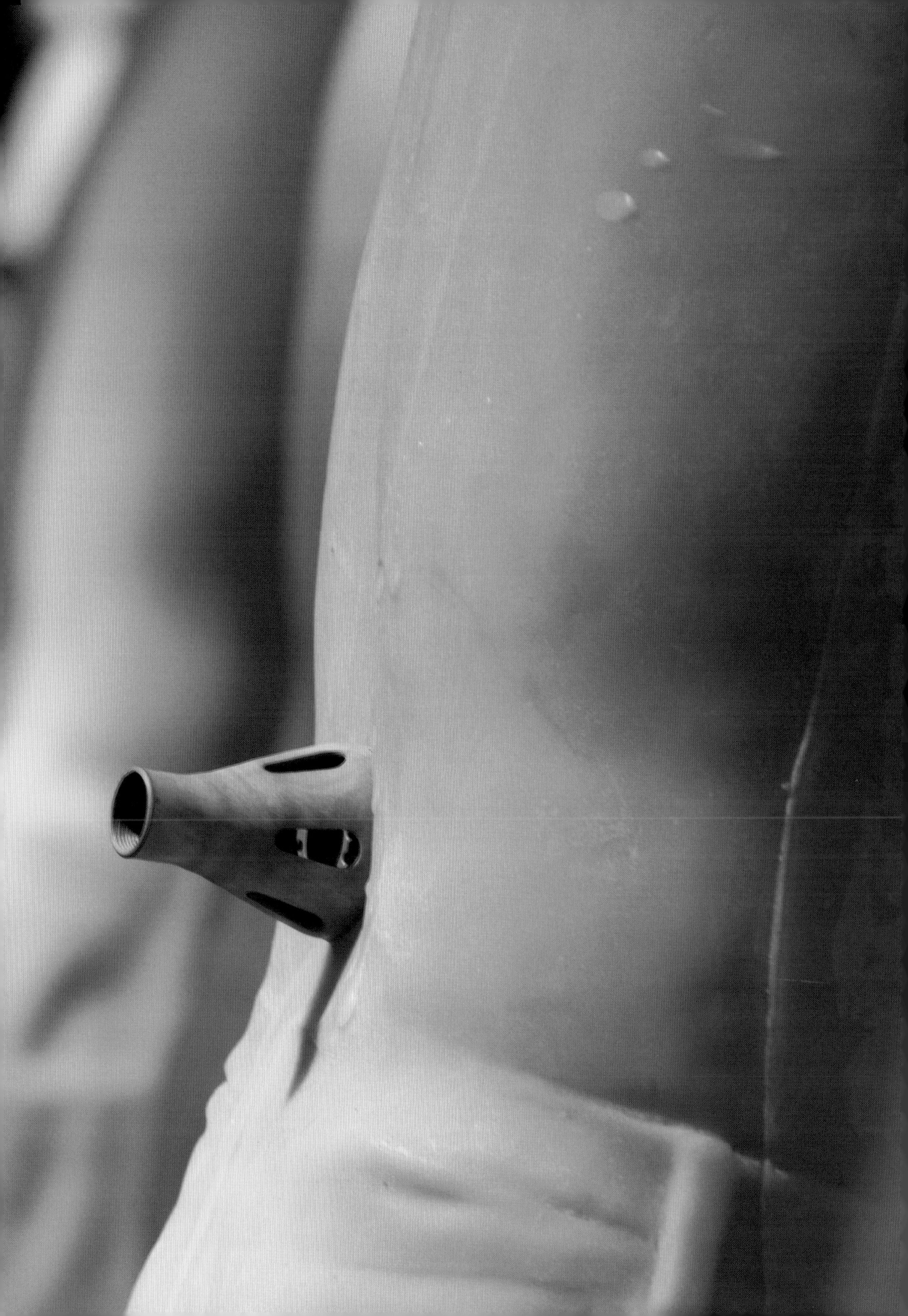

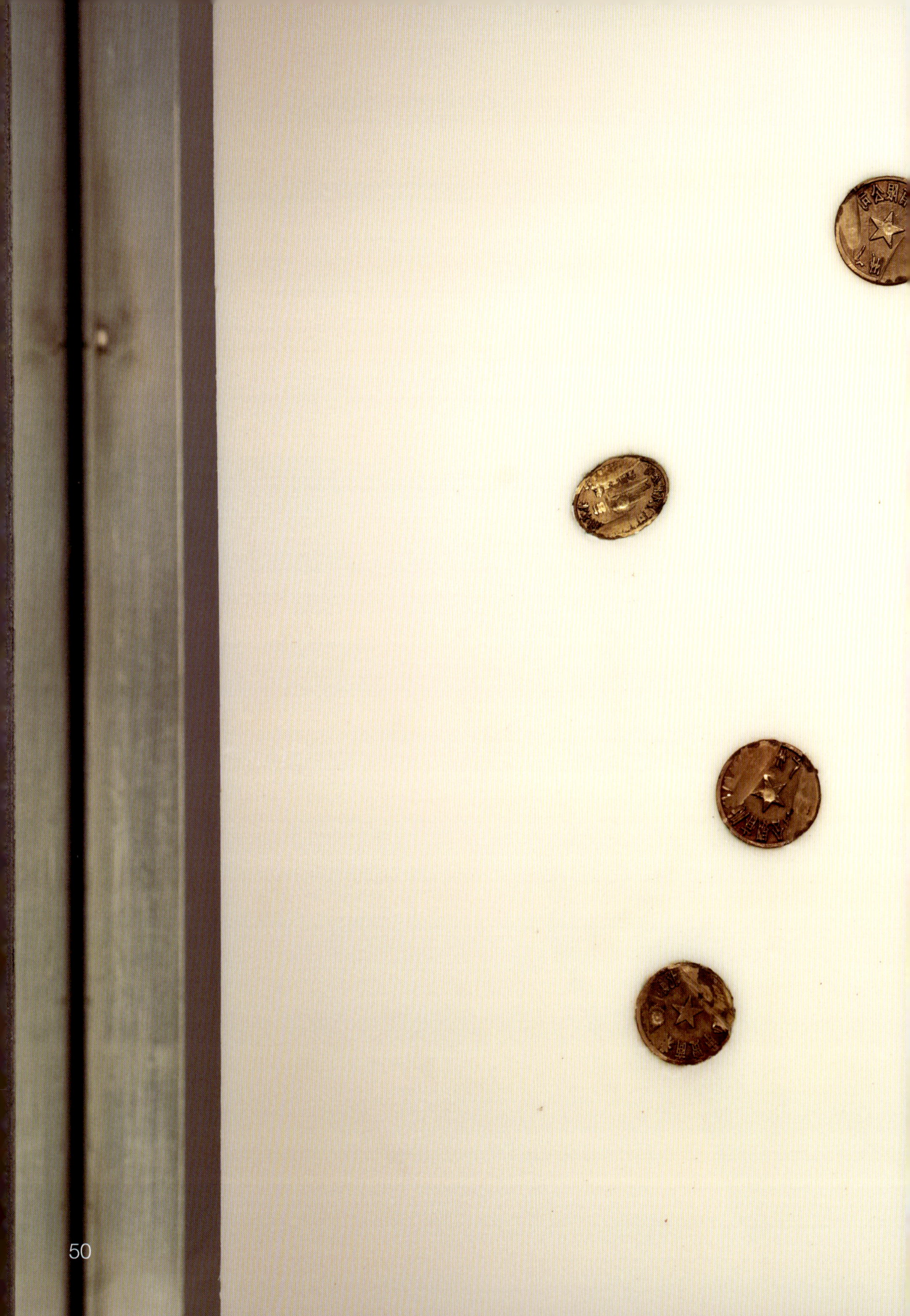

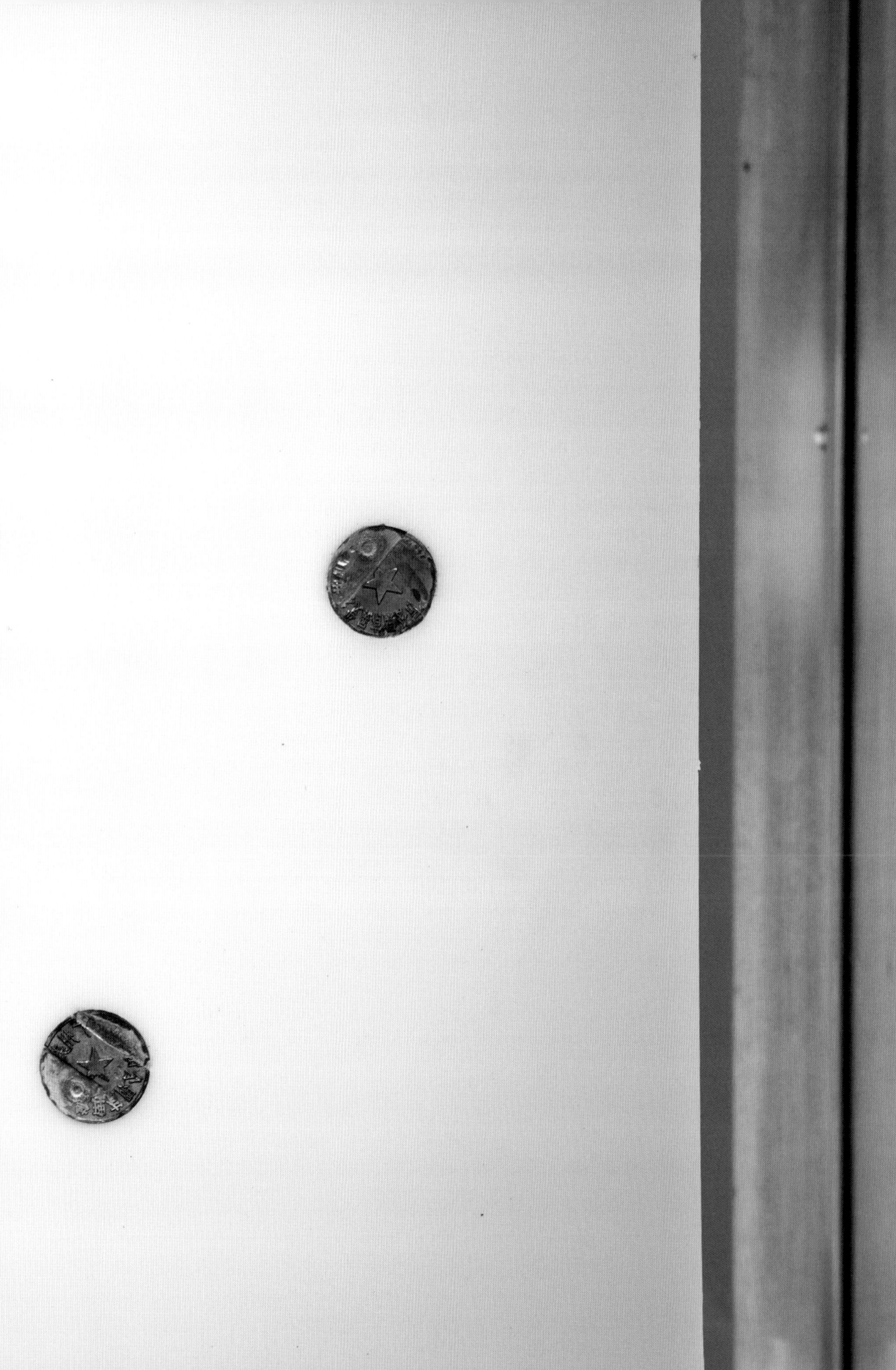

危的情绪注满。与之形成对比的，是我们在前文中讨论到的音频装置《苍蝇》里非常平静却持续的声音。不过，在这件作品中，黑暗的房间也营造出了一种不适和悬疑的感觉。

最后，作品《死亡是唯一的出口》会发出电击的声响，让我们的身体感受到轻微的震动。从上述讨论的作品可以看出，李怒的展览不仅为我们双眼提供了丰富的视觉盛宴，也在触觉和听觉上产生强烈的刺激。艺术家将身体视为和每一位观众共享的媒介，使之成为信息传递的有力工具：它不仅代表最个体化的经验，同时也强调了所有人之间的相似共性。他通过对自己身体的运用来提醒我们这种同一性：我们的命运紧密交织在一起。

拆解中心

《世界》这件作品重点讨论了有关"中心"的概念。在为作品调研的过程中，李怒意识到在许多文化的视觉历史、宗教以及精神传统中，普遍存在着单一起源说或是中心的概念。学者提图斯·布克哈德特（Titus Burckhardt）在谈到几个信仰传统时有相关的论述。例如北美苏族人的传统仪式中，他们以火坛定位四大方位以及大地和天空。这个祭坛被视为"世界的中心；然而事实上，这个中心无处不在，因为它也是精神的居所"。[19]也正由于这个观点无处不在，"仅是象征性引用就足以兑现现实效应"。[20]在中国古代传统的道家文化中，中心打孔通常是玉石材质的圆盘，便是非常常见的符号。布克哈德特写道，"这个玉盘象征着天或宇宙，中间的空无，则代表一种独特和超越的本质。"[21]而在基督教传统中，上帝被描述为："神就是一切，是开始、结尾和永恒的中心。"[22]鲁道夫·阿恩海姆（Rudolf Arnheim）提供了另一种谈论"中心"的方法——一种基于两种基本空间模式的视觉构成理论，他将其中一种称为同心或是宇宙中心。[23]作品《世界》亦从形式和观念两个角度展示了中心点的重要。

在李怒自己对此系列作品的陈述中，他提及古罗马建筑师、工程师维特鲁威（约公元前75—约公元前15）[24]在著作《建筑十书》中书写了人体比例的问题。维特鲁威解释道，人若将手脚伸展开来，那么，肚脐就在人体中心的位置。手脚不仅能画出一个圆圈，如果从头顶量到脚底，并且平移到伸长的手臂上，就在身体上画出了一个方形。[25]文艺复兴时期，维特鲁威的许多构想被建筑师、艺术家和工程师所采纳，其中达·芬奇著名的《维特鲁威人》便是源于此。李怒还提到古罗马人建城前先标明城市中心点的方法——这个中心点被称为"世界"，即上文提到的城市与神明的连接点，地下天上皆然。他在作品《世界》研究式的介绍中总结道："相传罗穆卢斯在公元前753年4月21日于帕拉丁山丘挖掘了一个'世界'，创建了罗马。"

《世界》展示了一位模特背部和脐部的细微运动，李怒解释道，他创作这个视频意在"厘清人与自然、城市和世界的原初关联"。他写道，"人有自己的中心（即肚脐），（它）也是世界的中心，人即世界。"[26]

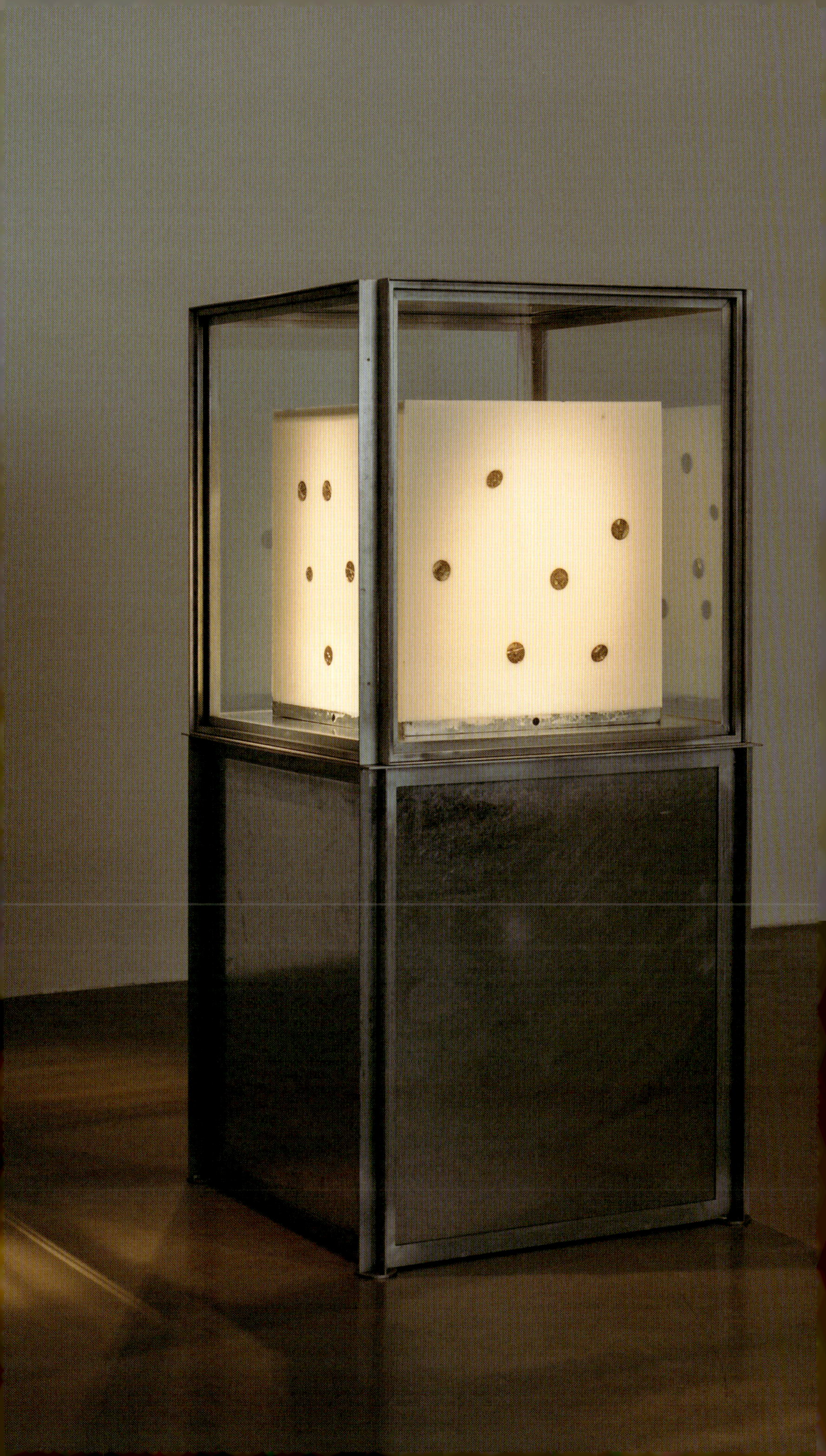

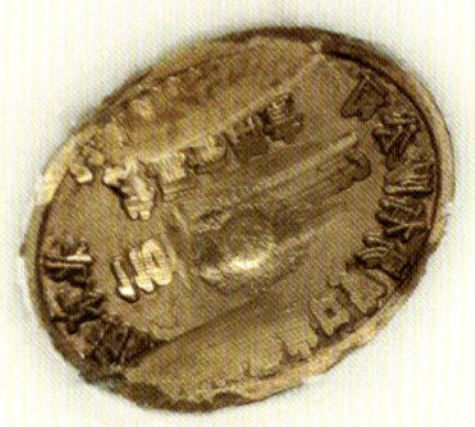

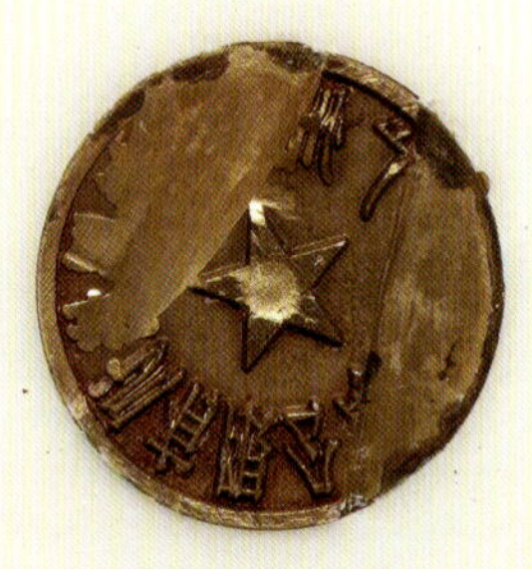

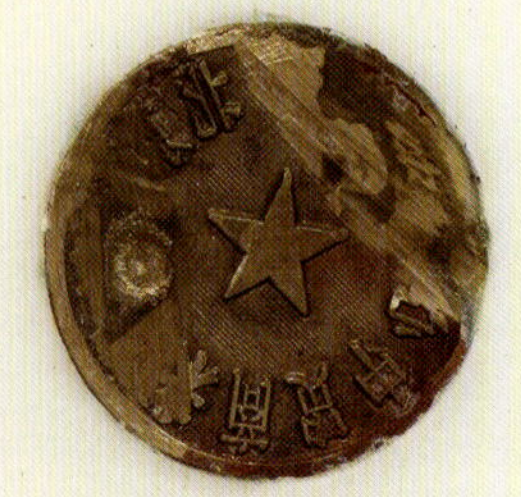

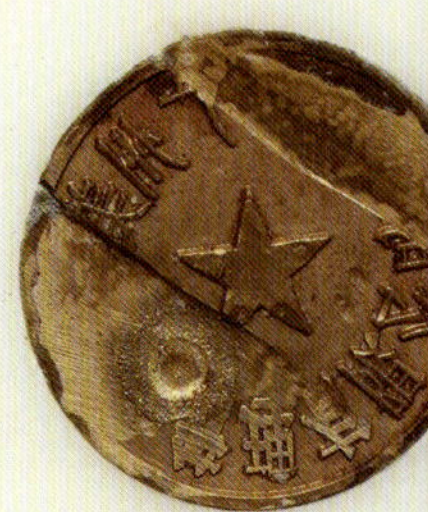

结语

在李怒的首个机构个展中，大量作品呈现出丰富的视觉词汇和对于媒介、材料的多样化使用，这不仅仅是一个视觉盛宴，也在测探我们听觉和触觉的回应。他提出了一种替代性和意想不到的方式来审视世界各地人们面临的社会政治问题。也许在这个展览中，我们很难将李怒的艺术归类为某种特定的风格或媒介，但其中反复出现了一些重要元素，例如文字——不论是受到文学、歌词还是双关语启发，出现在以文本为基础的作品、展览标题还是作品的标题。这是李怒作品的重要面向，也是他在传达的关键信息。以文本为基础的创作也让艺术家得以并置、建立起东西方哲学中重叠地带的联系。传统媒介和非常规媒材的使用都能延长作品在象征意义上表达的深度和广度。他运用身体——确切来说，是他自己的身体——作为若干作品的出发点来表达一种具有共性的领会，这是将我们人类连接在一起的东西。最后，他引入"中心"的重要性——在作品形式和观念上皆有涉猎，这是自古以来便存在于不同文化和传统中的强大符号。正是通过上述四个基础，李怒得以熔炼出一系列创作，从而反思这个动荡时代的普世关切。

---

[1]出自《经外福音书片断》。首次出版的译文如下："磐石上的建筑是没有的，所有建筑的根基都在沙上，我们的责任是建筑时要把沙当成磐石。"博尔赫斯，《为六弦琴而作·影子的颂歌》，林之木、王永年译（上海：上海译文出版社，2016），第118页。博尔赫斯的这首诗似乎是对圣经《马太福音》第五章第五节中的著名经文"温柔的人有福了"所做的讽喻。 [2] KIKIlllly 对李怒的采访，《李怒：来自寂静的见证》，"艺文力"微信公众号，2022年11月11日发布。 https://mp.weixin.qq.com/s/FF88Qs9Nq4a4HOpAgx9iIg.。 [3] 李怒与作者的谈话。 [4] https://en.wikisource.org/wiki/The_Complete_Short_Stories_of_Guy_de_Maupassant/Ball-of-Fat.。 [5]同上。 [6]而萨特的《苍蝇》则改编自古希腊经典悲剧《厄勒克特拉》。 [7]李怒与作者的谈话。 [8]见艺术家对《硬陛》的作品陈述。 [9]同上。 [10]《楞伽经·刹那品第六》（北京：中华书局，2010），第198页。 [11] https://terracottaarmychina.com/is-there-really-mercury-in-the-underground-palace-of-qin-shihuangs-mausoleum. [12]《李怒：来自寂静的见证》。 [13] 艺术家对《世界》的创作陈述。 [14] 《李怒：来自寂静的见证》。 [15] 同上。 [16] 同上。 17 李怒与作者的谈话。 [18] 艺术家对《庇护所》的创作陈述。 [19] 参见：Titus Burckhardt, 'The Universality of Sacred Art', The Essential Titus Burckhardt: Reflections on Sacred Art, Faiths, and Civilizations, ed. by William Stoddart (Bloomington: World Wisdom, 2003), p. 97. [20] 同上，第98页。 [21] 同上，第105页。 [22] 同上，第111页。 [23] 参见：The Power of the Center: A Study of Composition in the Visual Arts (1982). 第二种中心则是笛卡尔或网格体系的中心概念。 [24] 见艺术家对《世界》的陈述。 [25] 参见：维特鲁威《建筑十书·第三书》第一章第三节，高履泰译（北京：知识产权出版社，2001），第71—72页。 [26] 见艺术家对《世界》的陈述。

恩睦哲，是一位写作者、作家和策展人，现居多伦多。她于2005年至2023年间在北京生活时，为《Frieze》《ArtAsiaPacific》和《ARTOMITY》等出版物撰写了大量评论、艺术家访谈及专题报道，关注中国当代艺术。自2017年起，她便长期关注李怒的艺术创作。目前，她为关注BIPOC艺术的杂志《Rungh》撰稿。她是姜涛、爱德华 W. 姜合著《父与子：绘画是生命的绵延》（河北美术出版社，2023）的英文编辑。与乔·卡特合著有《巴哈伊灵曦堂：设计、建造与社群》（牛津乔纳·罗纳德出版社，2022）。展览图录文章包括：《森林小丘——冯良鸿个展》（北京三远当代艺术，2022），《法利·阿吉拉尔：历史在召唤》（北京马刺画廊，2021），《和谐与时间的考验：向阳的幻化之屋在日本越后妻有大地艺术节》（2018）。她策划了冯志佳个展"迷迭"（北京EGG画廊，2023）。她与高毅共同策划了克里斯蒂娜·库比施个展"电子漫步"（上海UN Art跨媒体艺术中心，2018）。

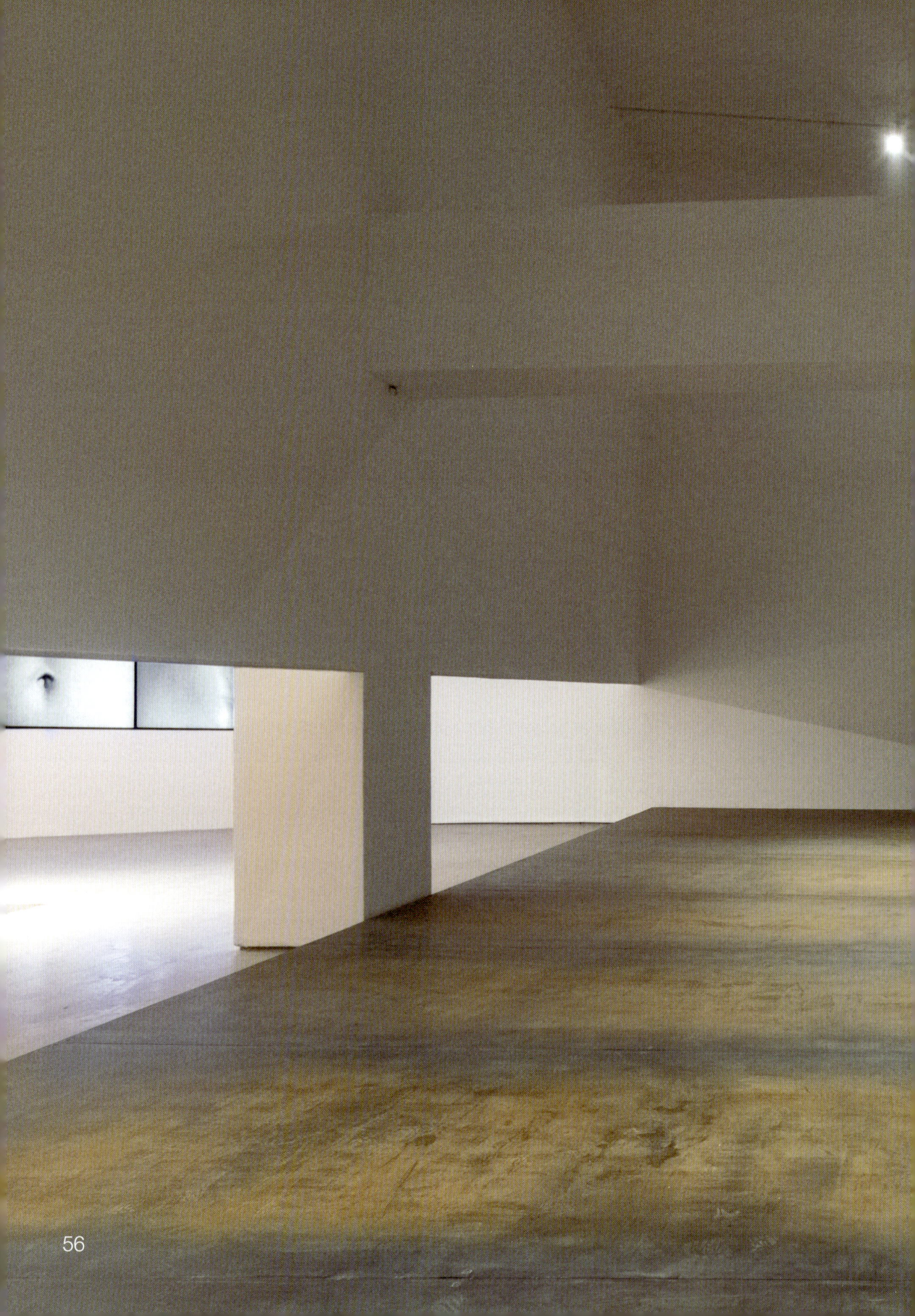

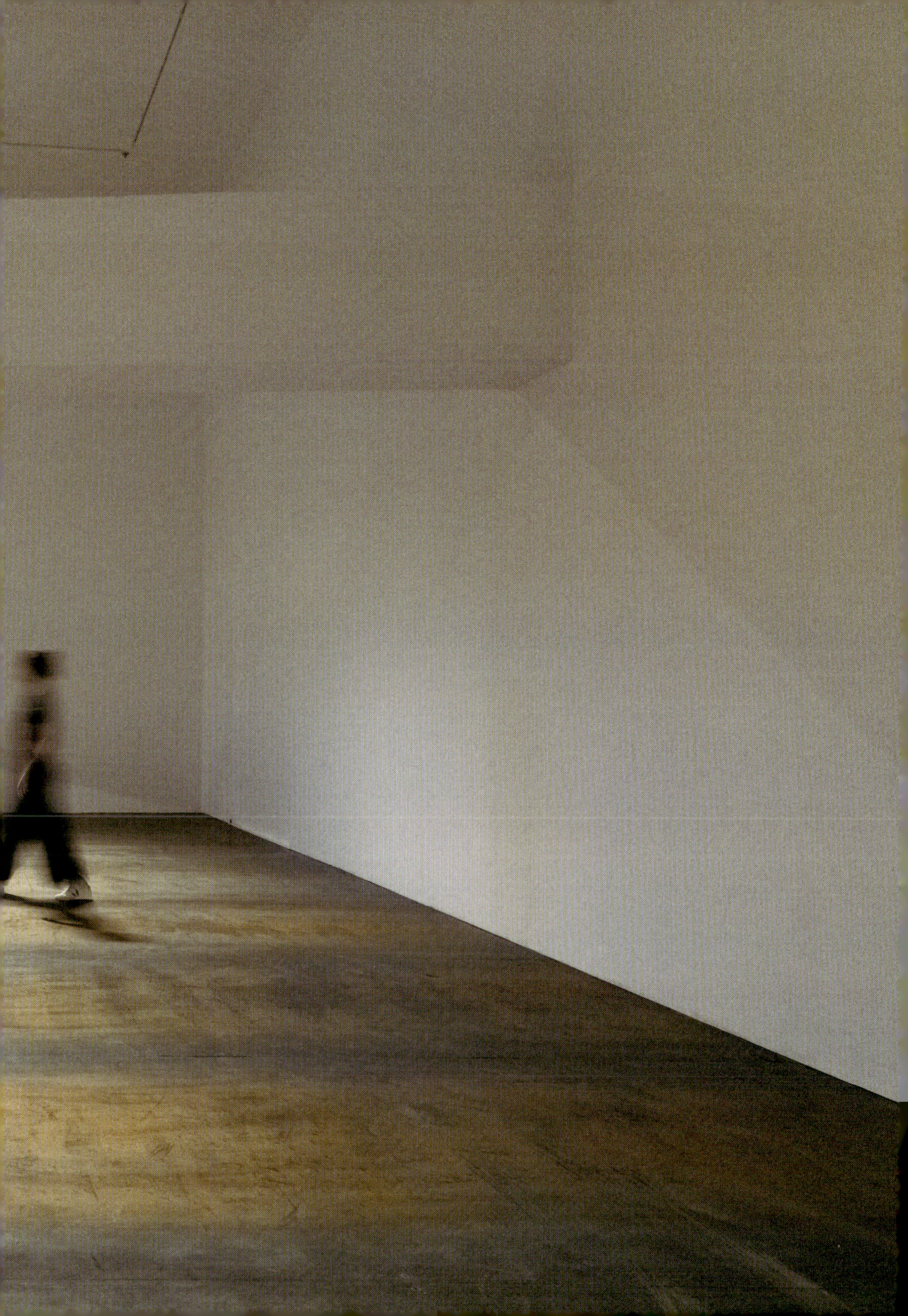

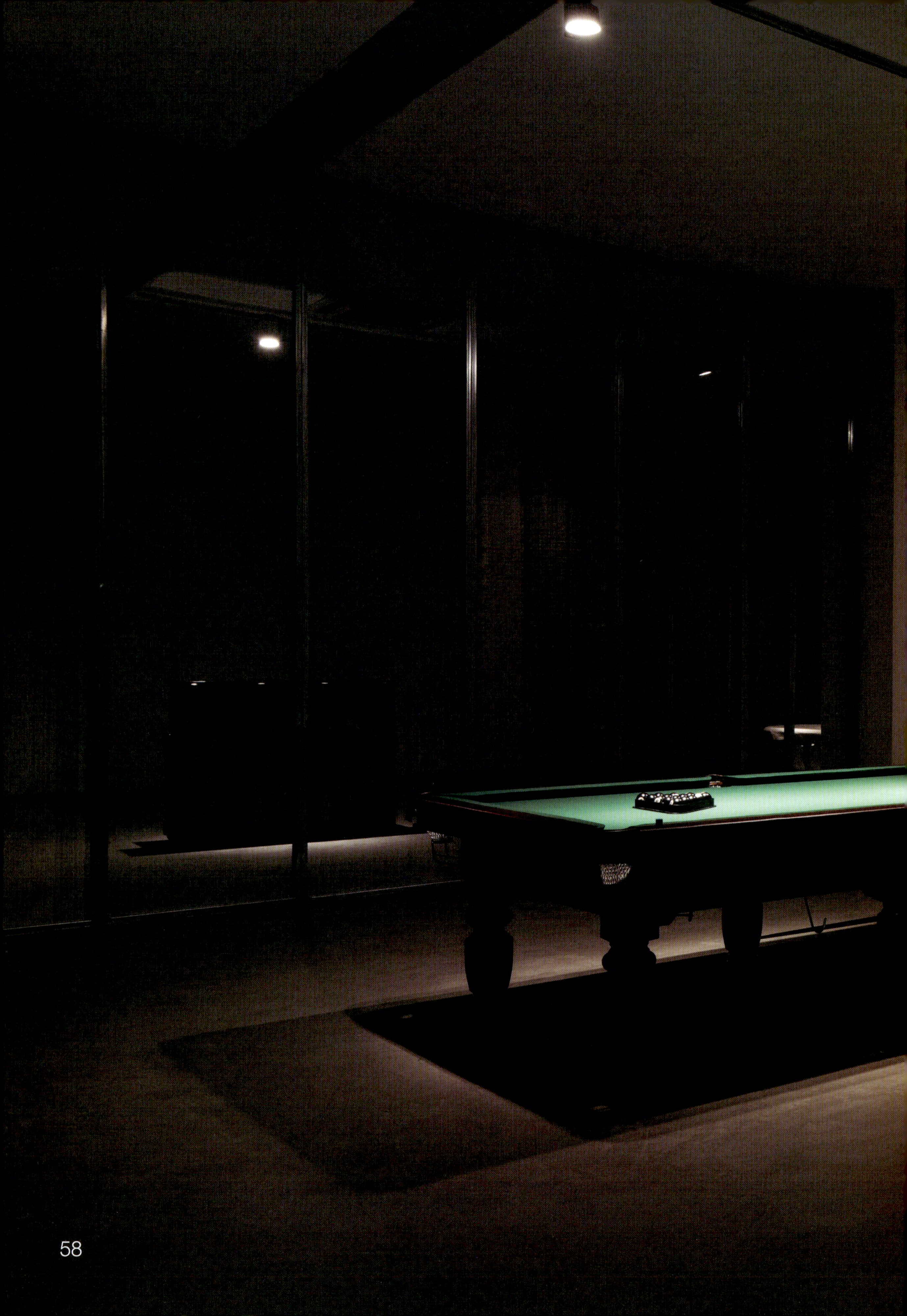

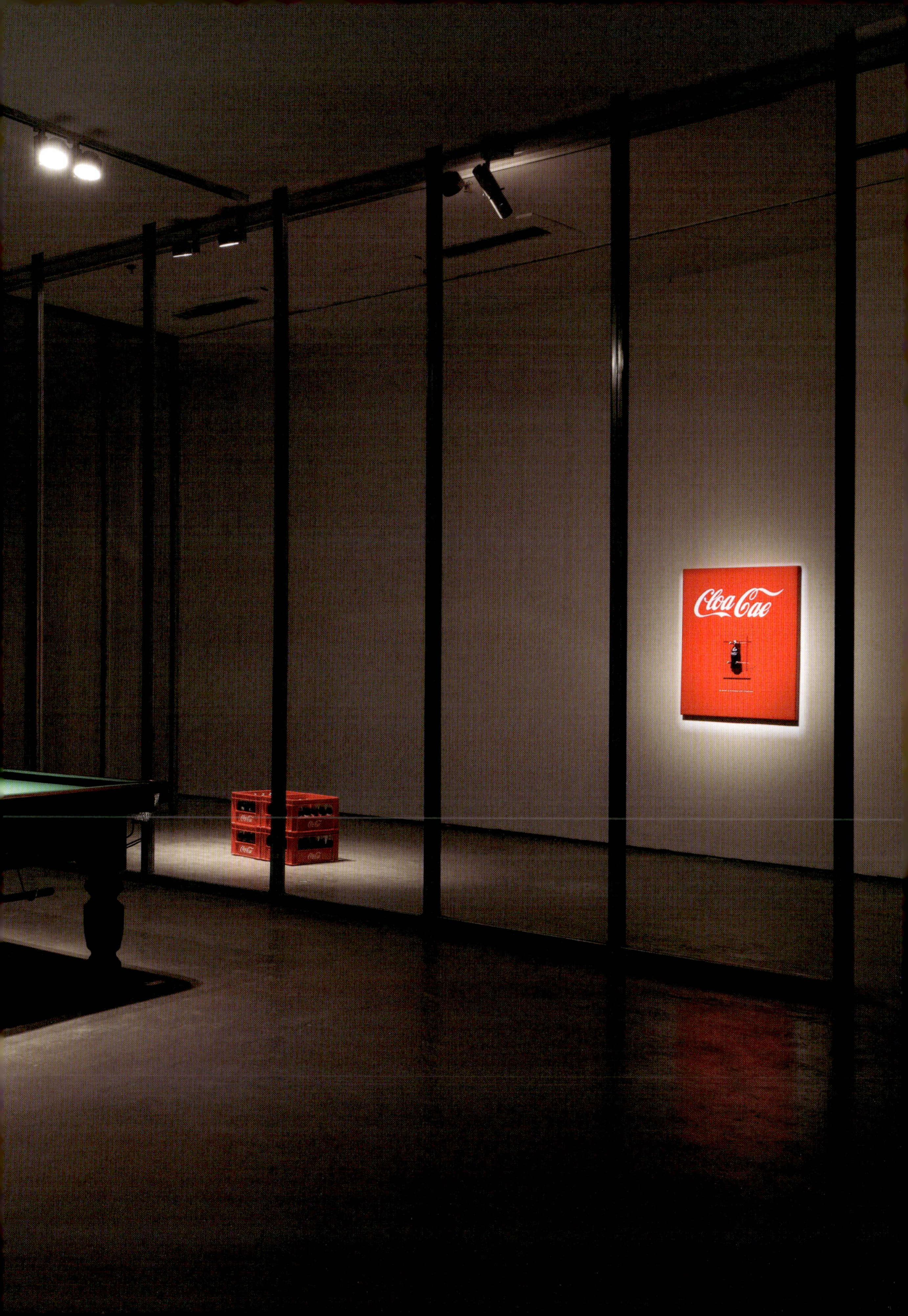

Cloa Cae

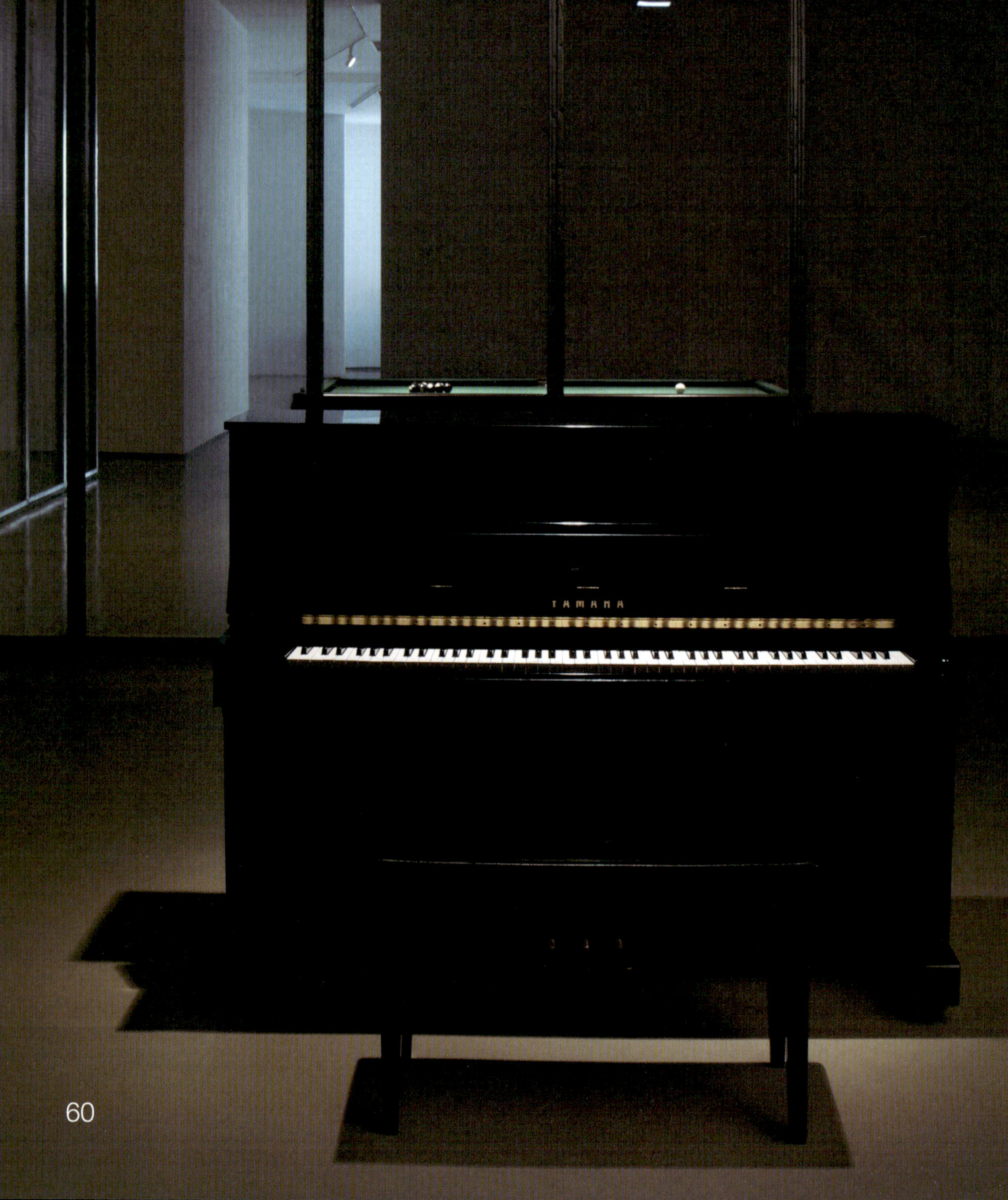
YAMAHA

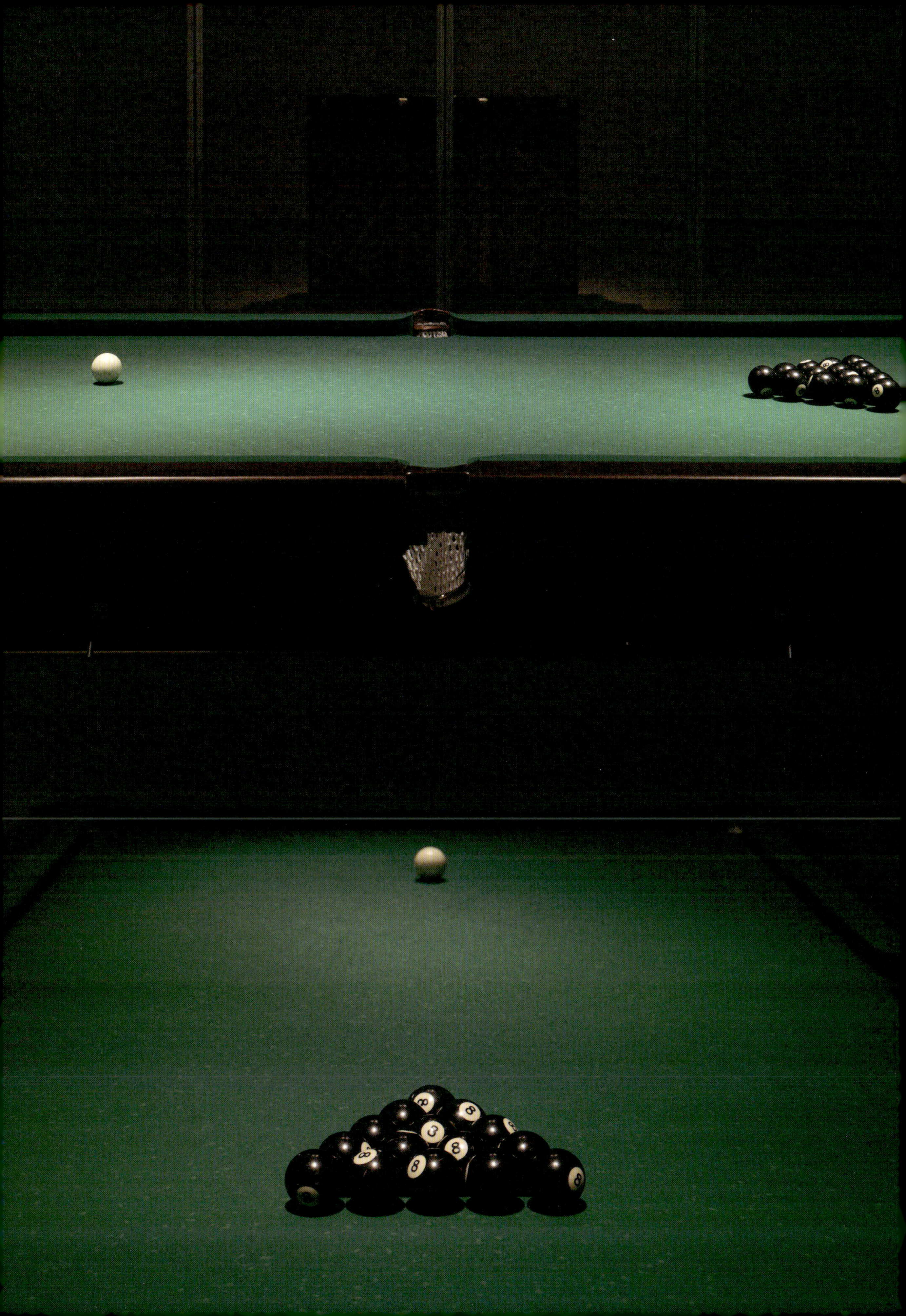

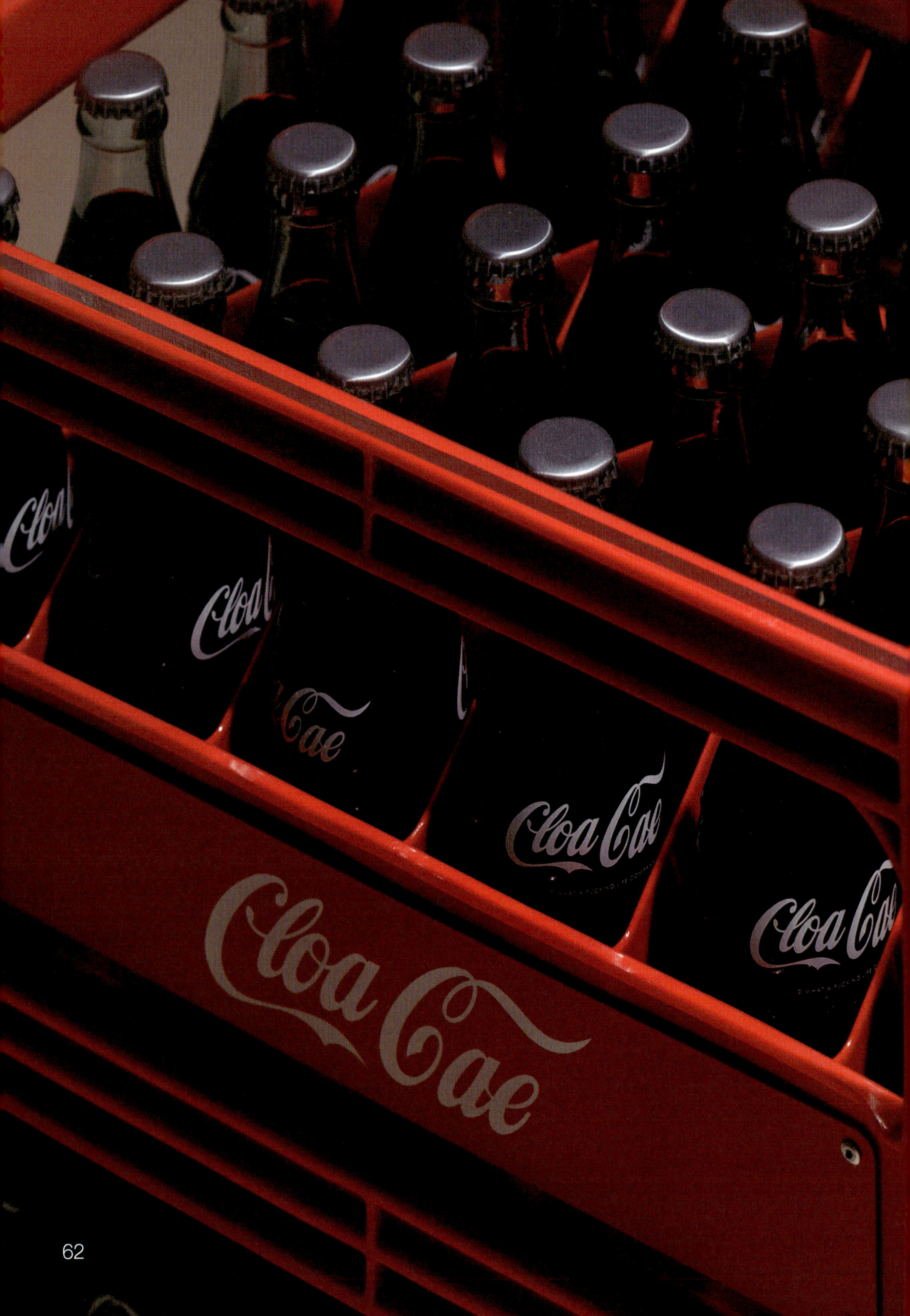

Cloa Cae
Cloa Cae
Cloa Cae
Cloa Cae

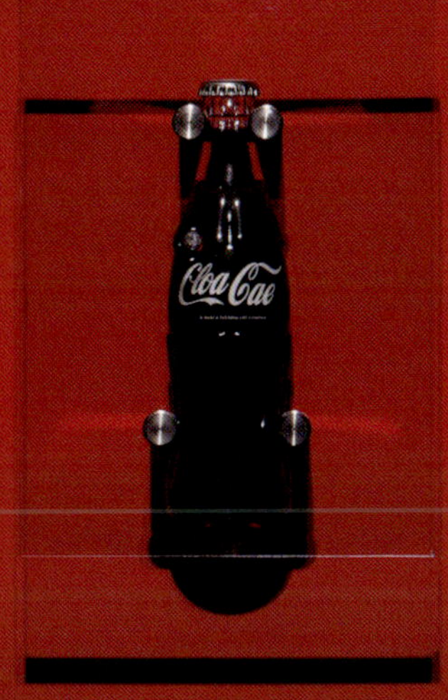

© WHAT A FUCKING LIFE COMPANY

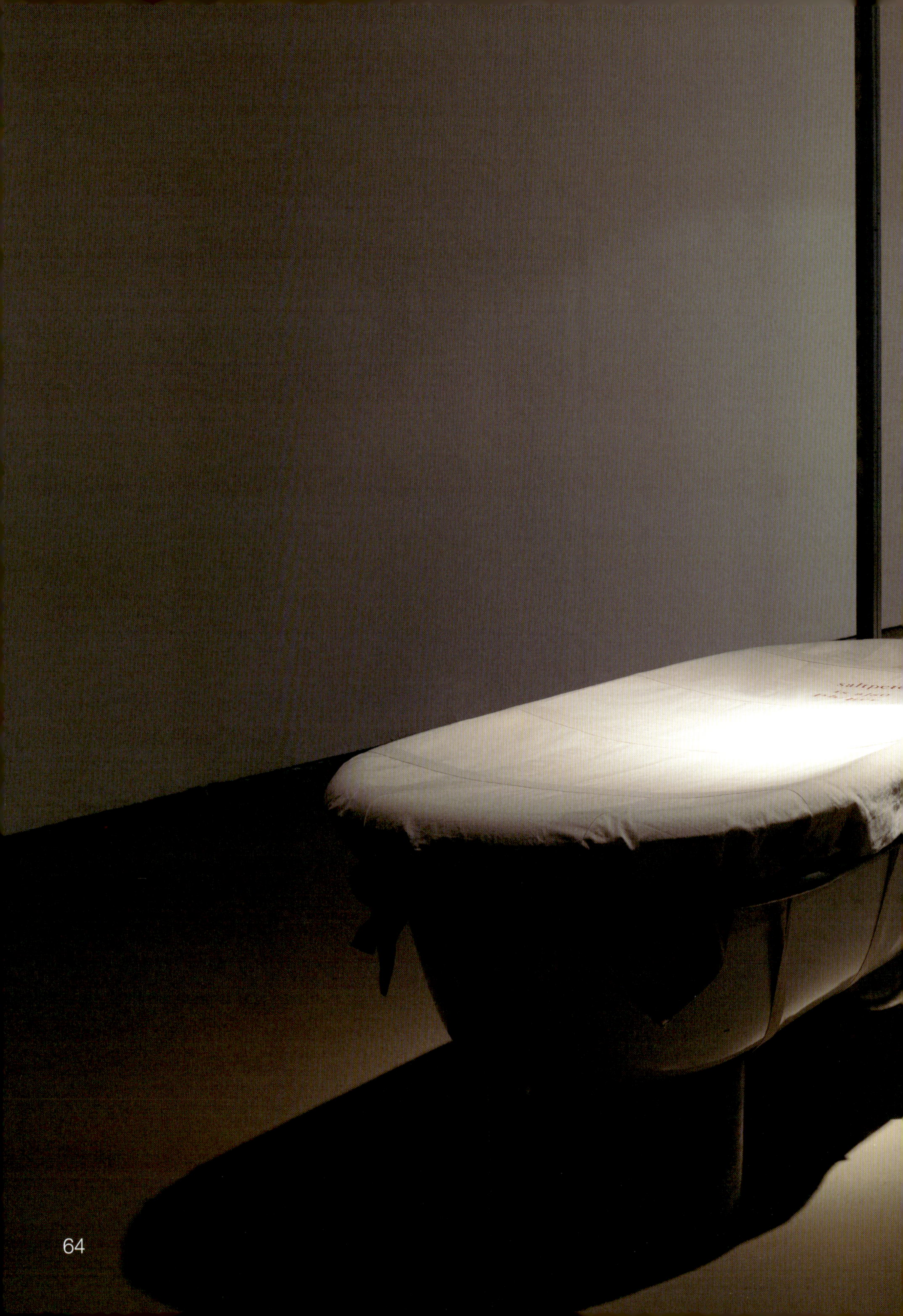

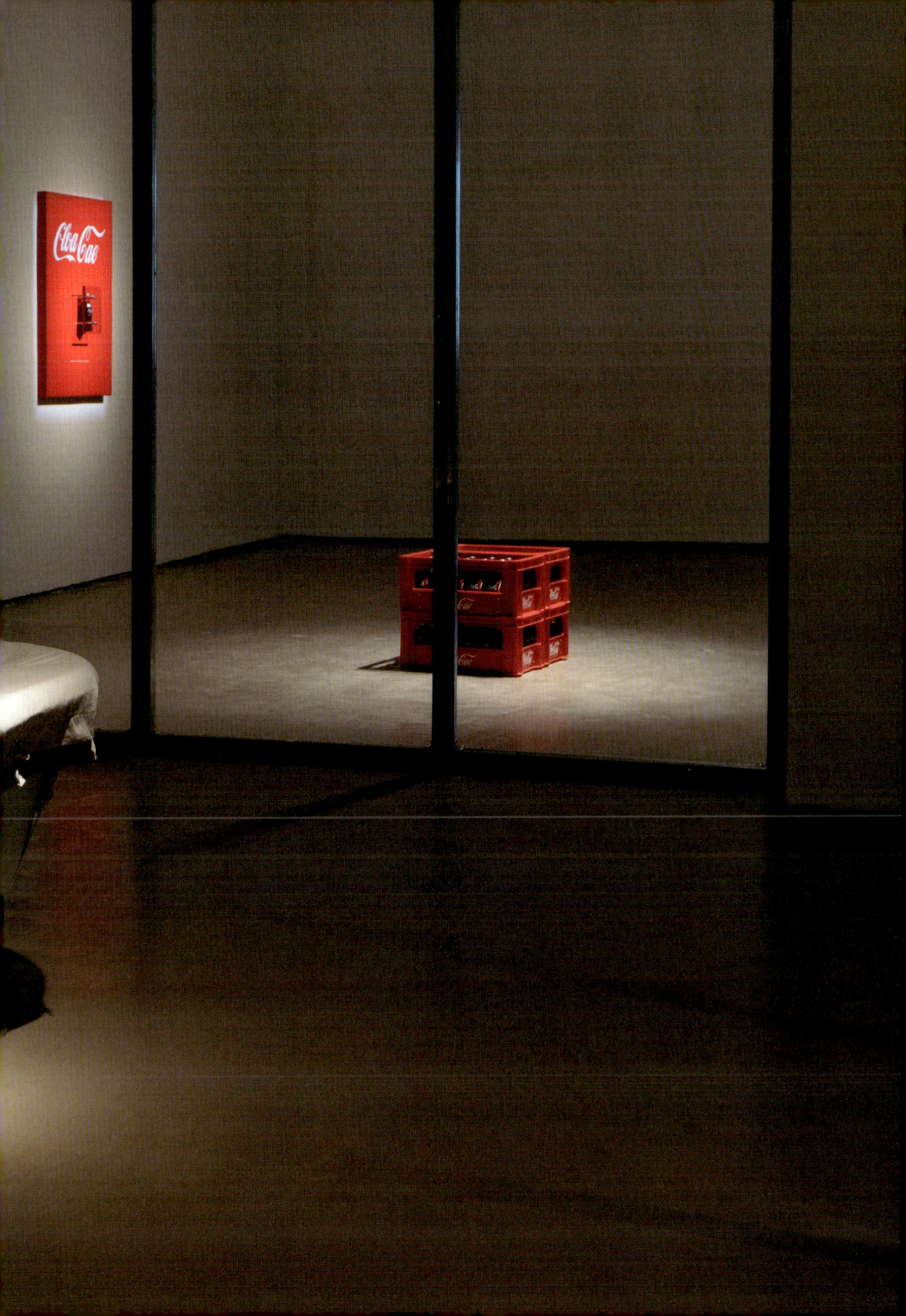

Coca Cola

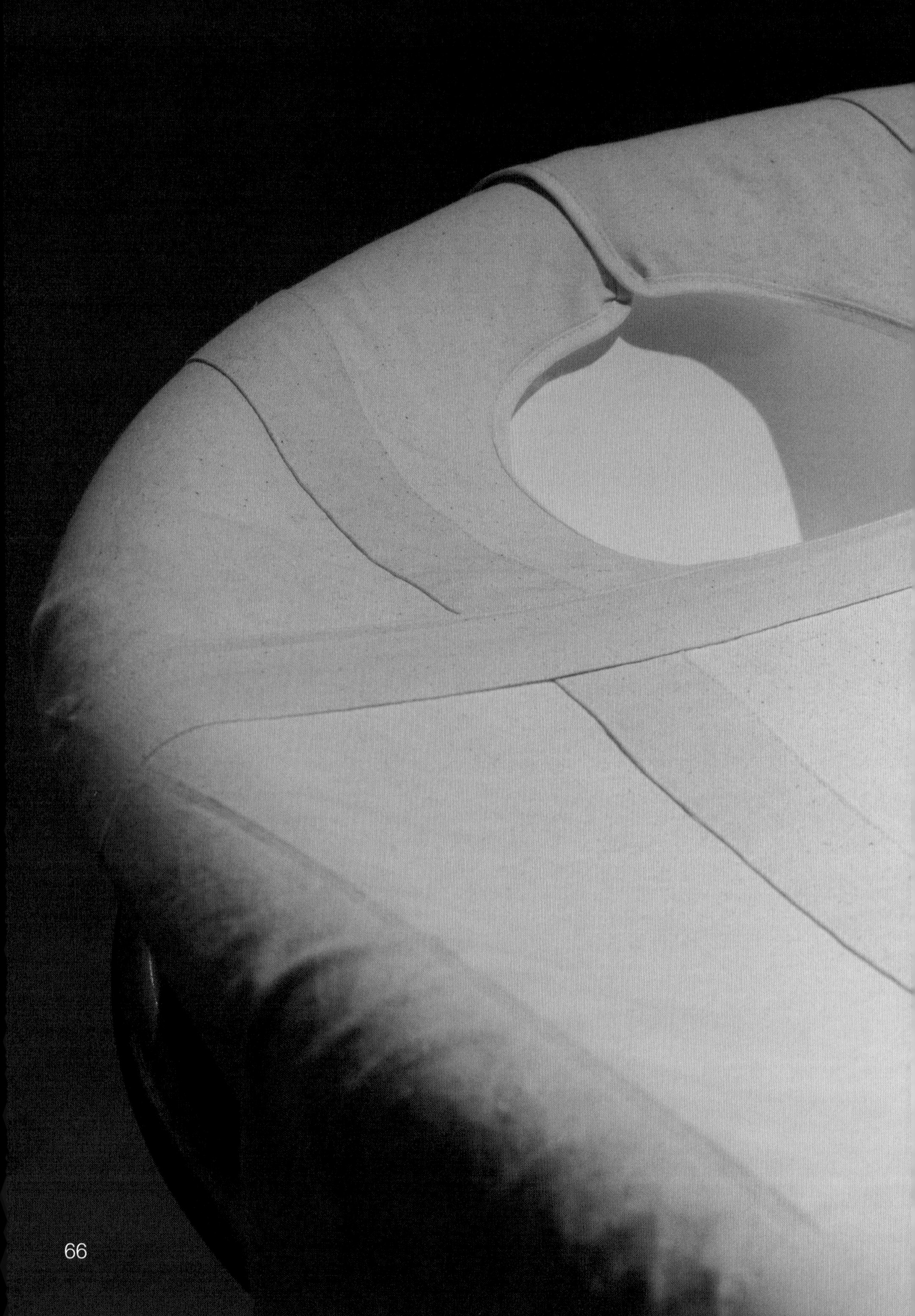

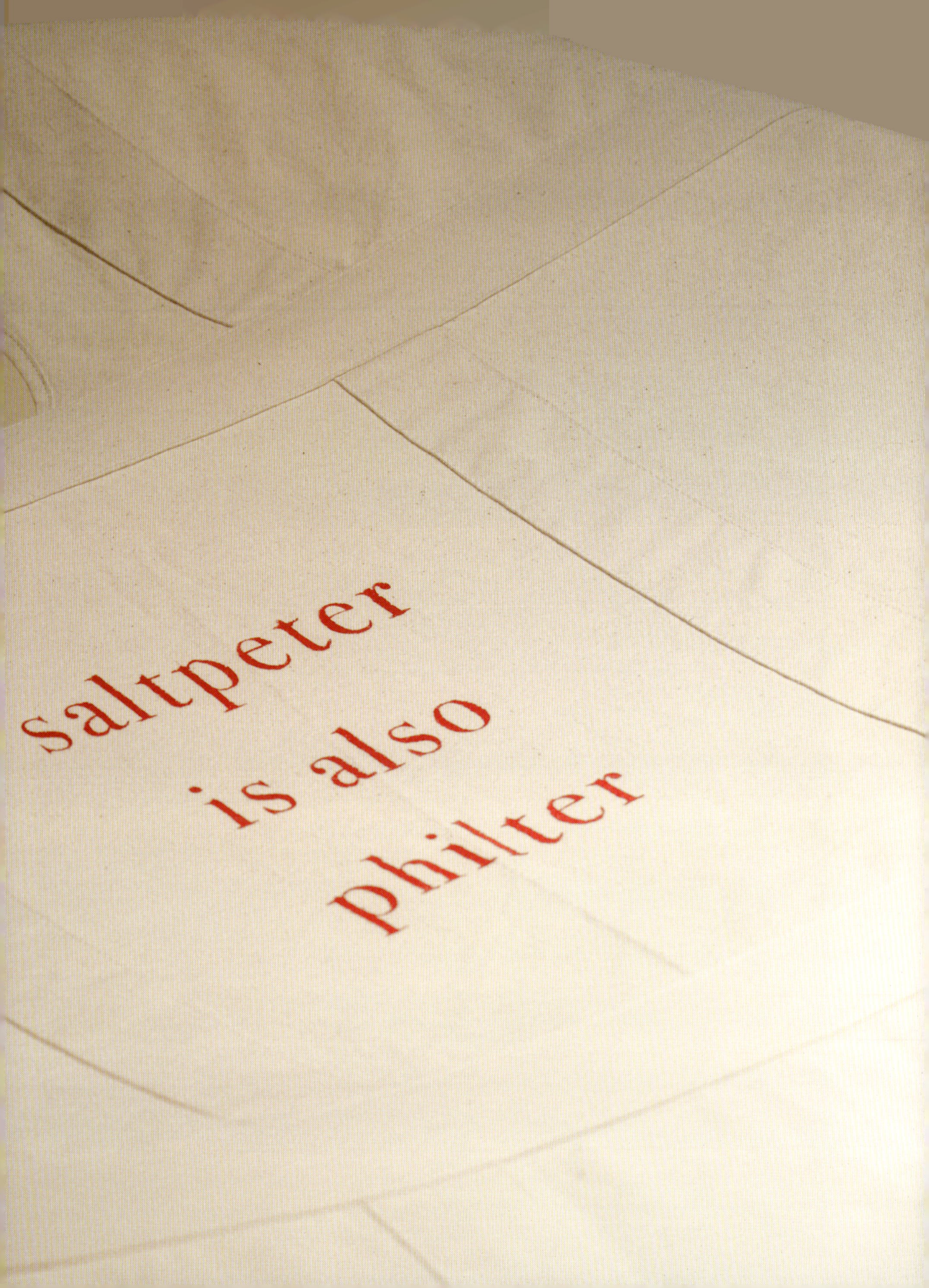

saltpeter
is also
philter

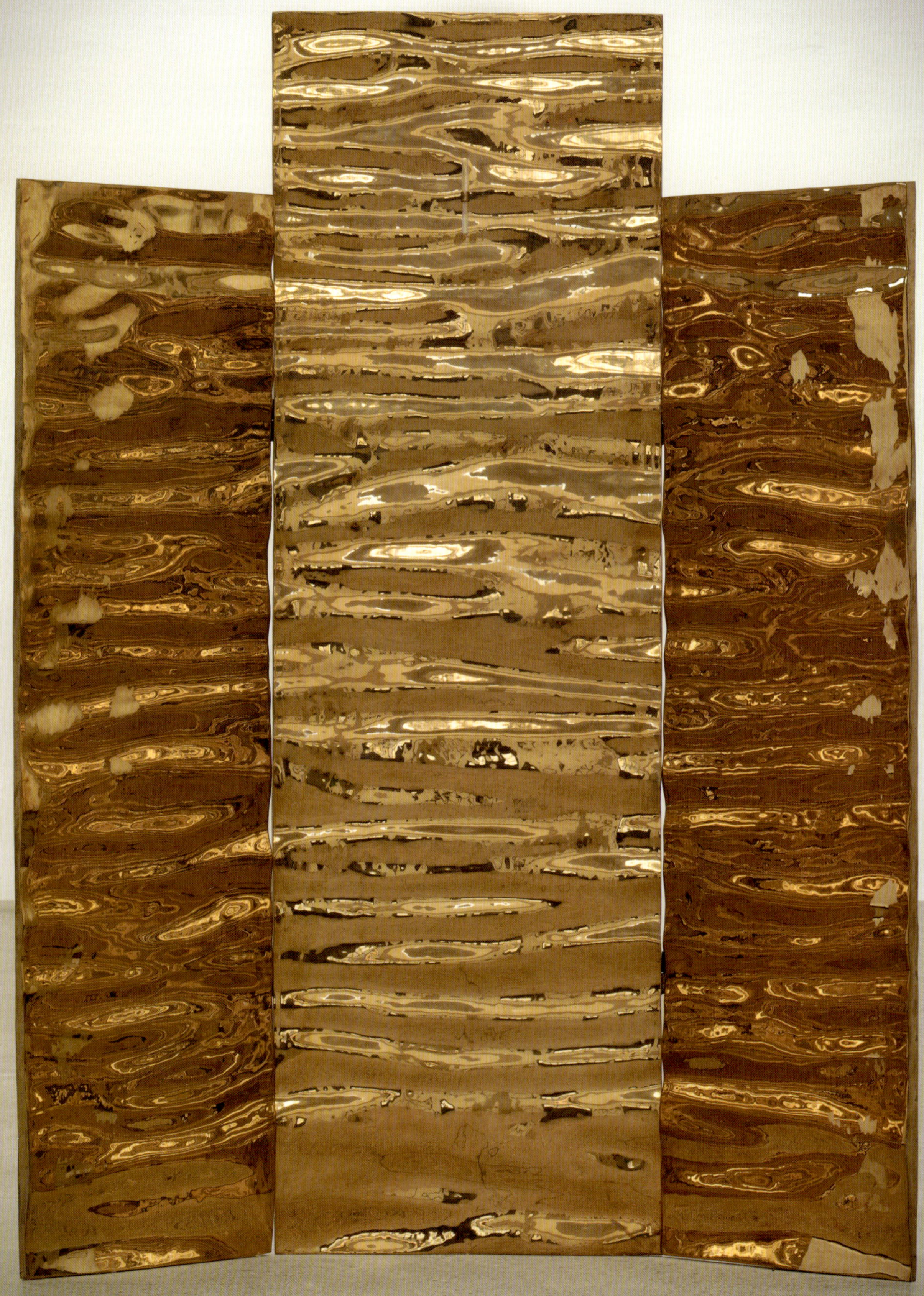

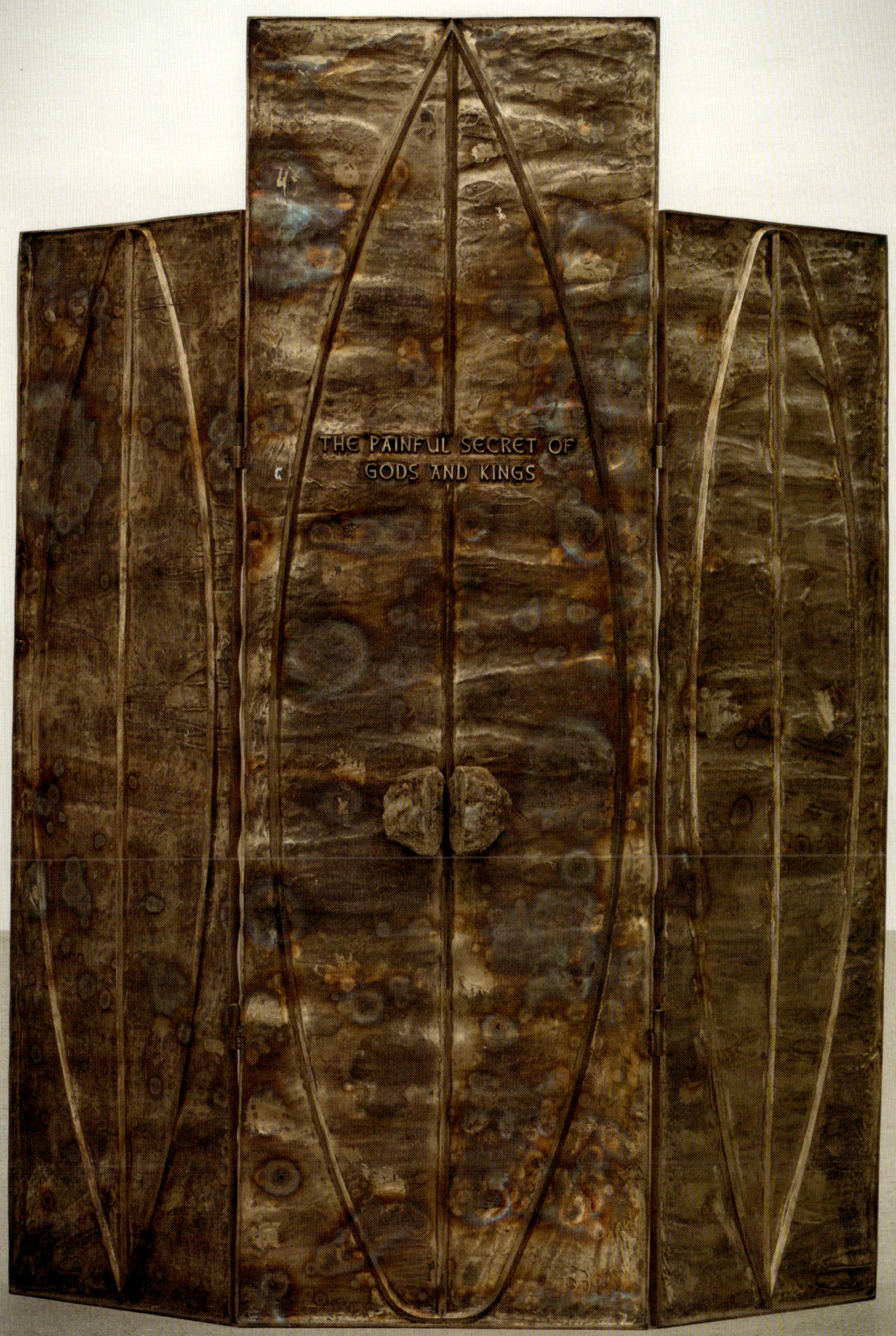

THE PAINFUL SECRET OF
GODS AND KINGS

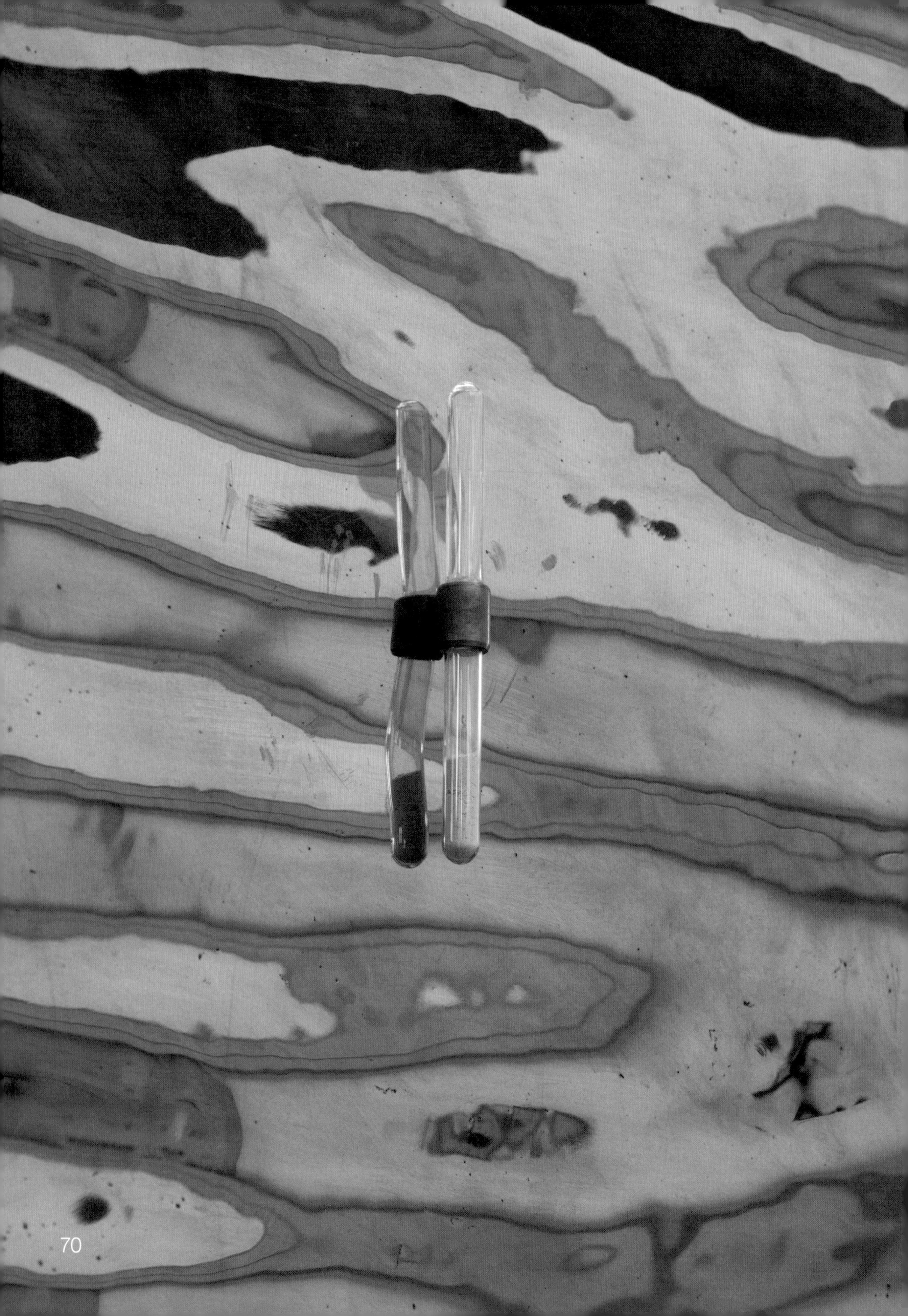

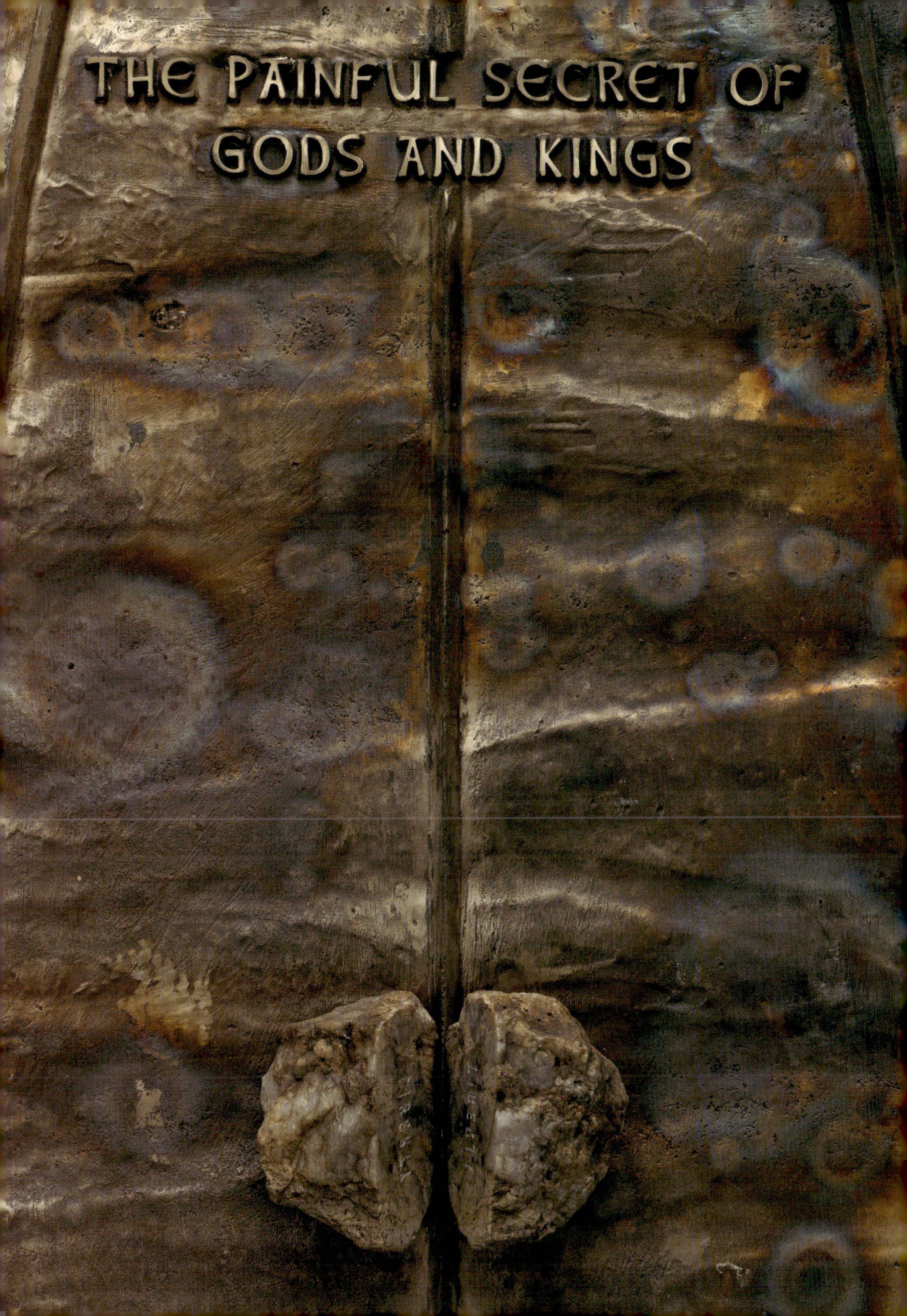

THE PAINFUL SECRET OF
GODS AND KINGS

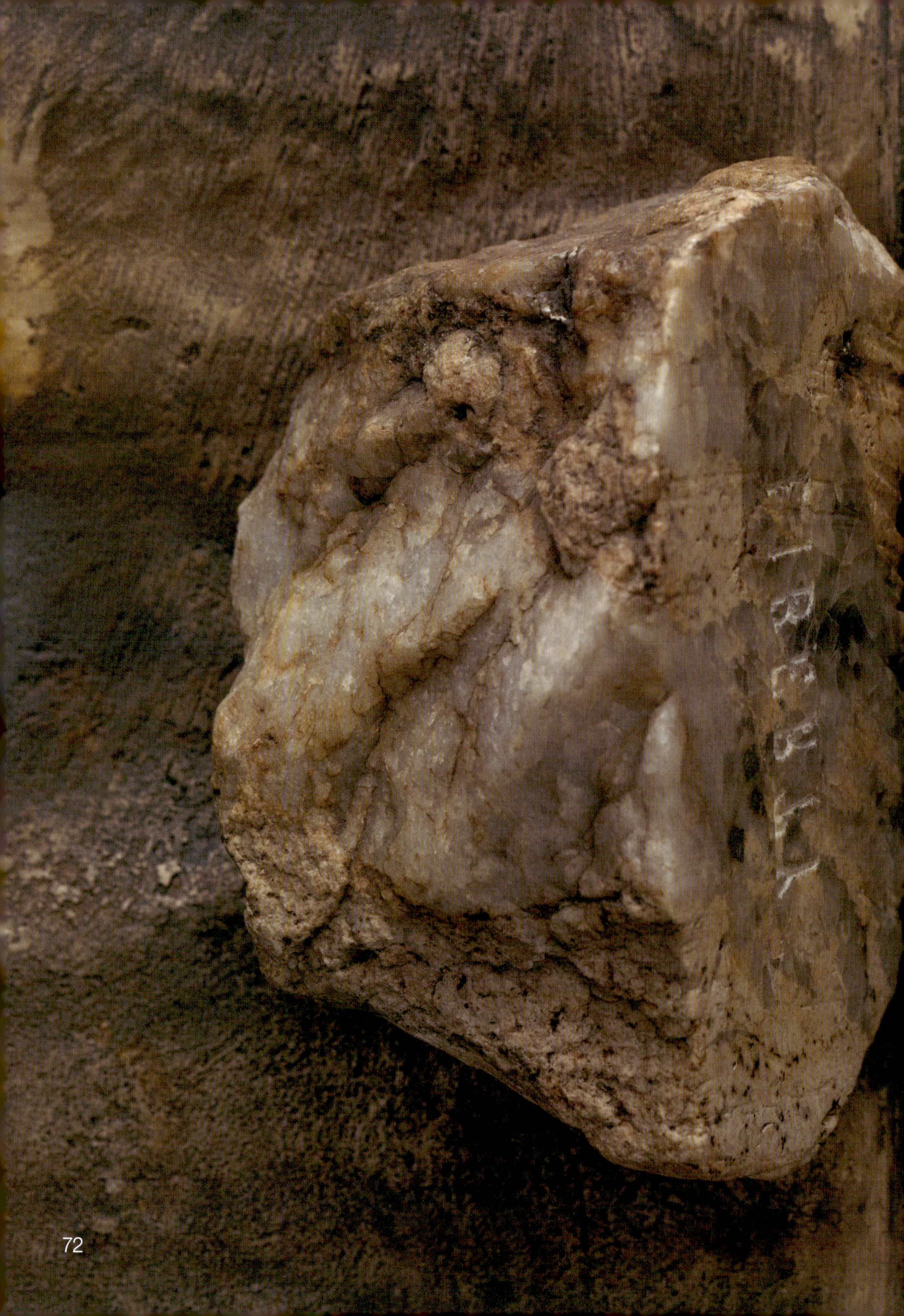

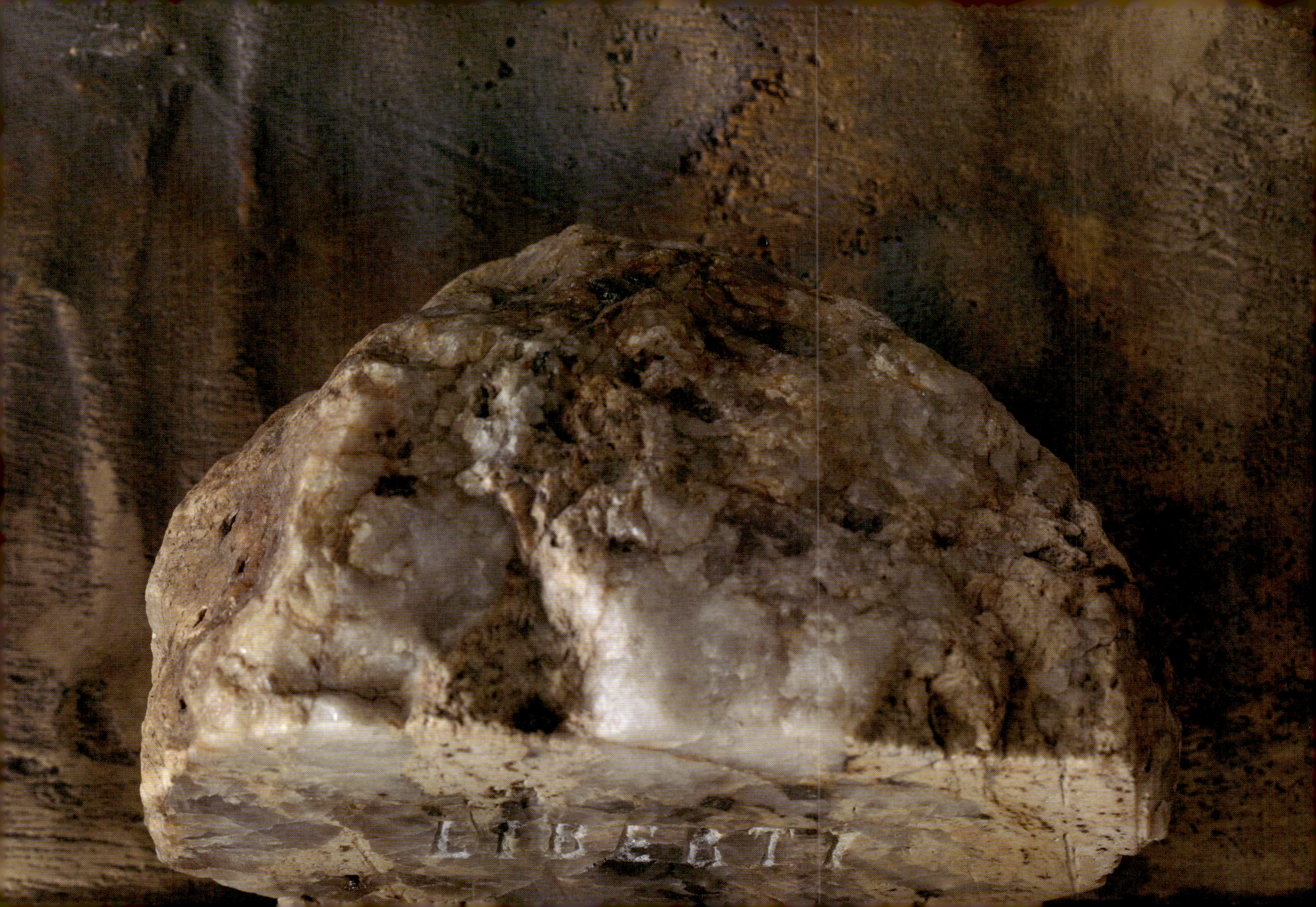
LIBERTY

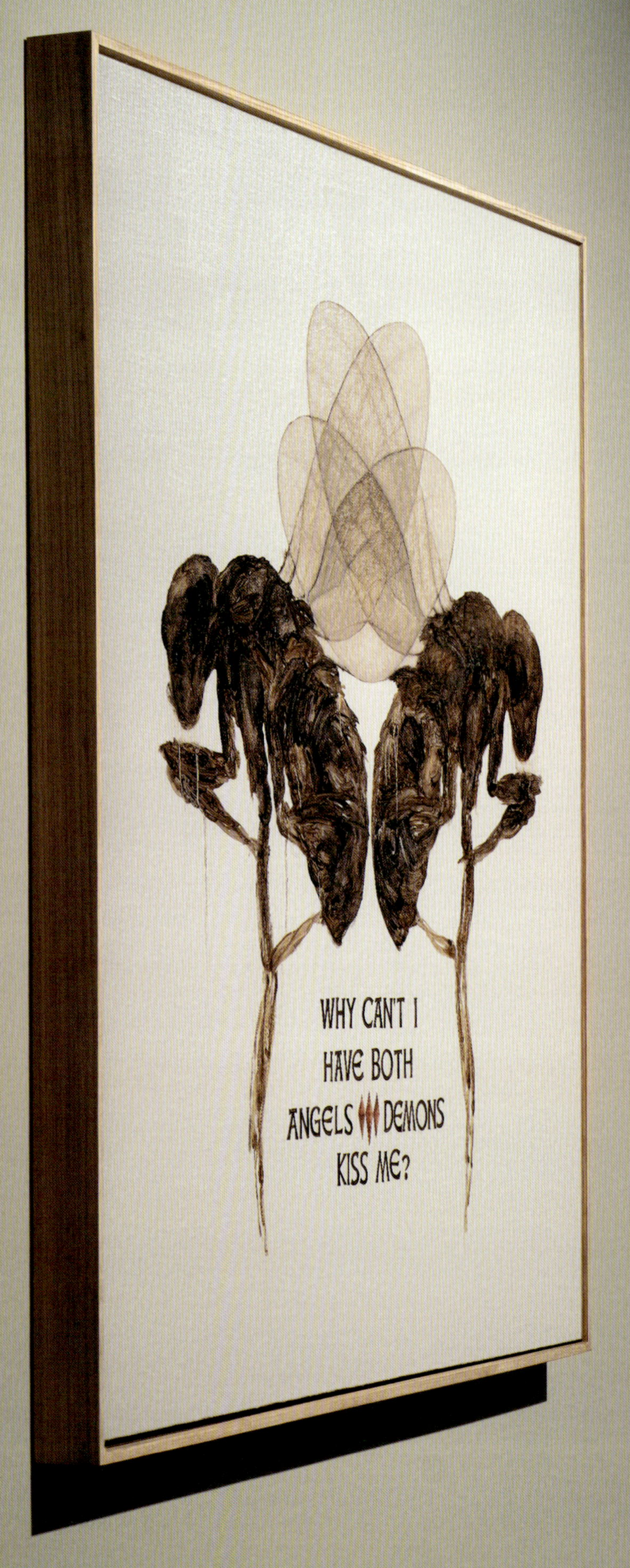

WHY CAN'T I
HAVE BOTH
ANGELS & DEMONS
KISS ME?

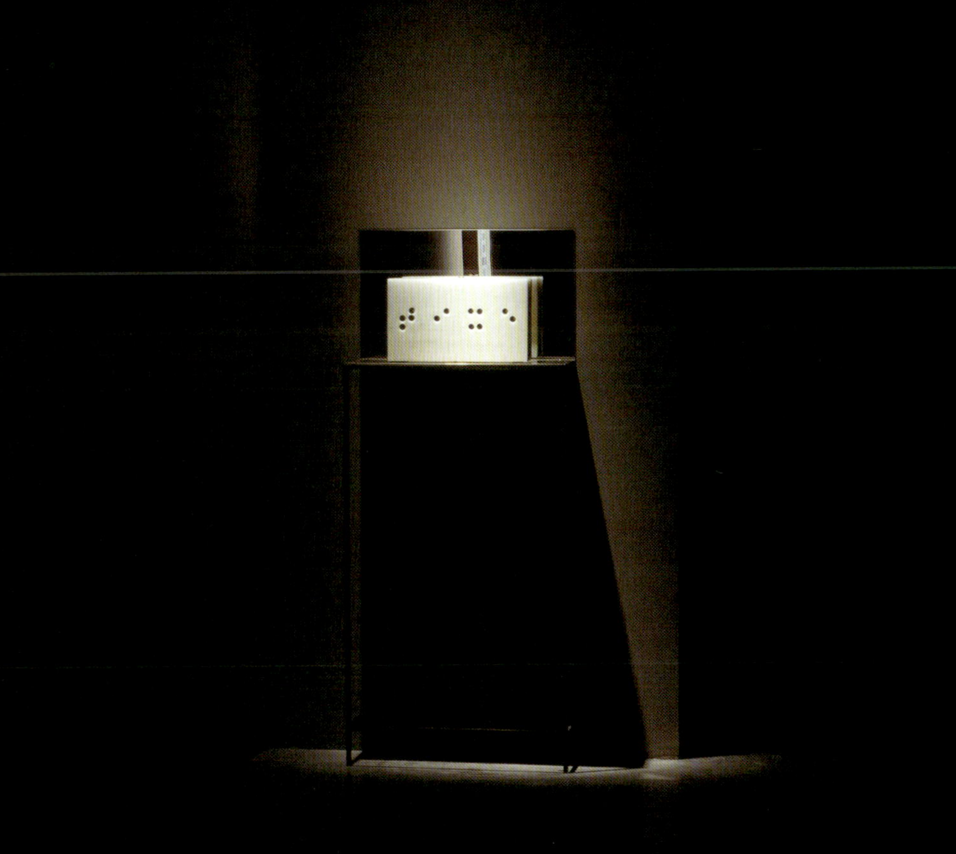

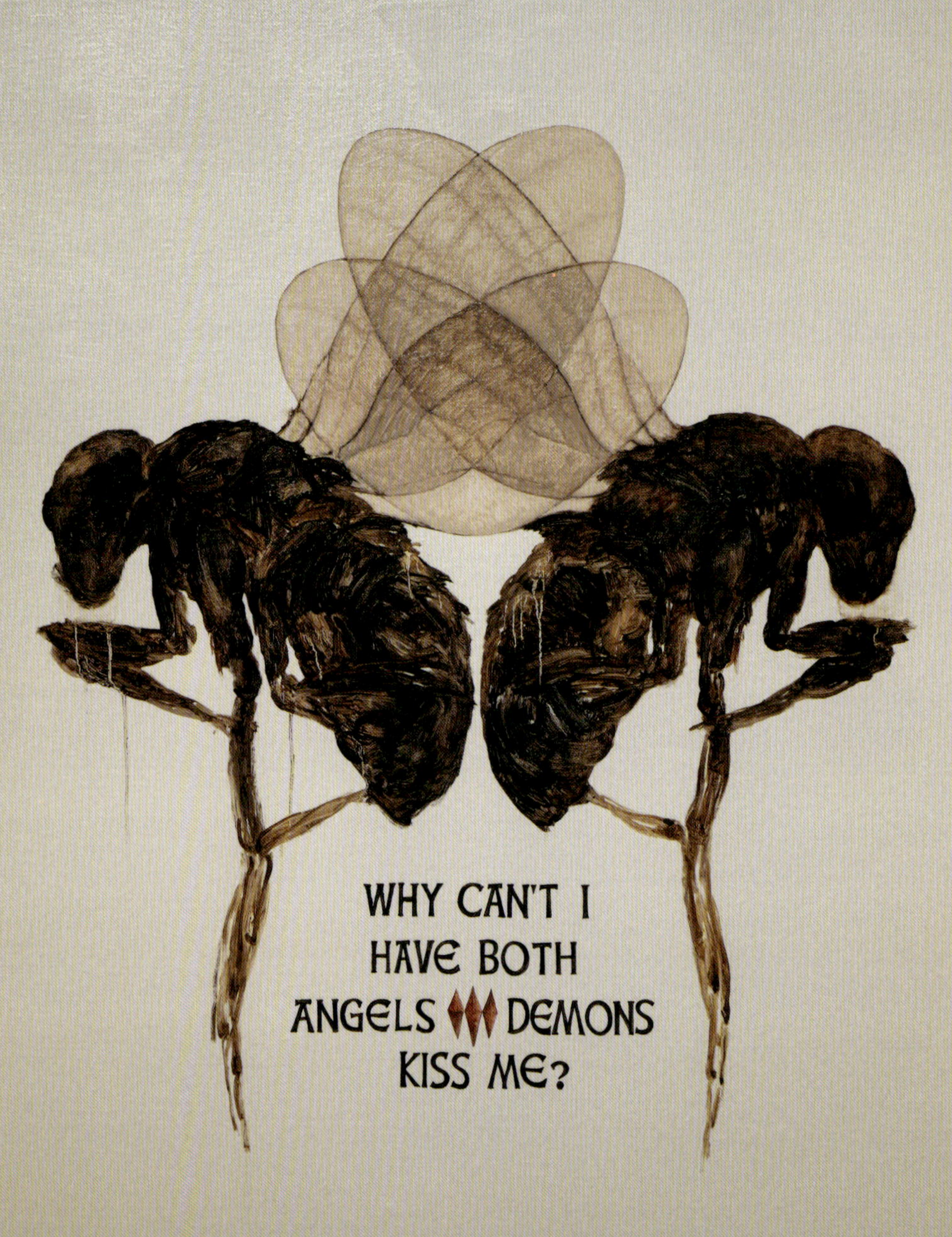

WHY CAN'T I
HAVE BOTH
ANGELS ❖ DEMONS
KISS ME?

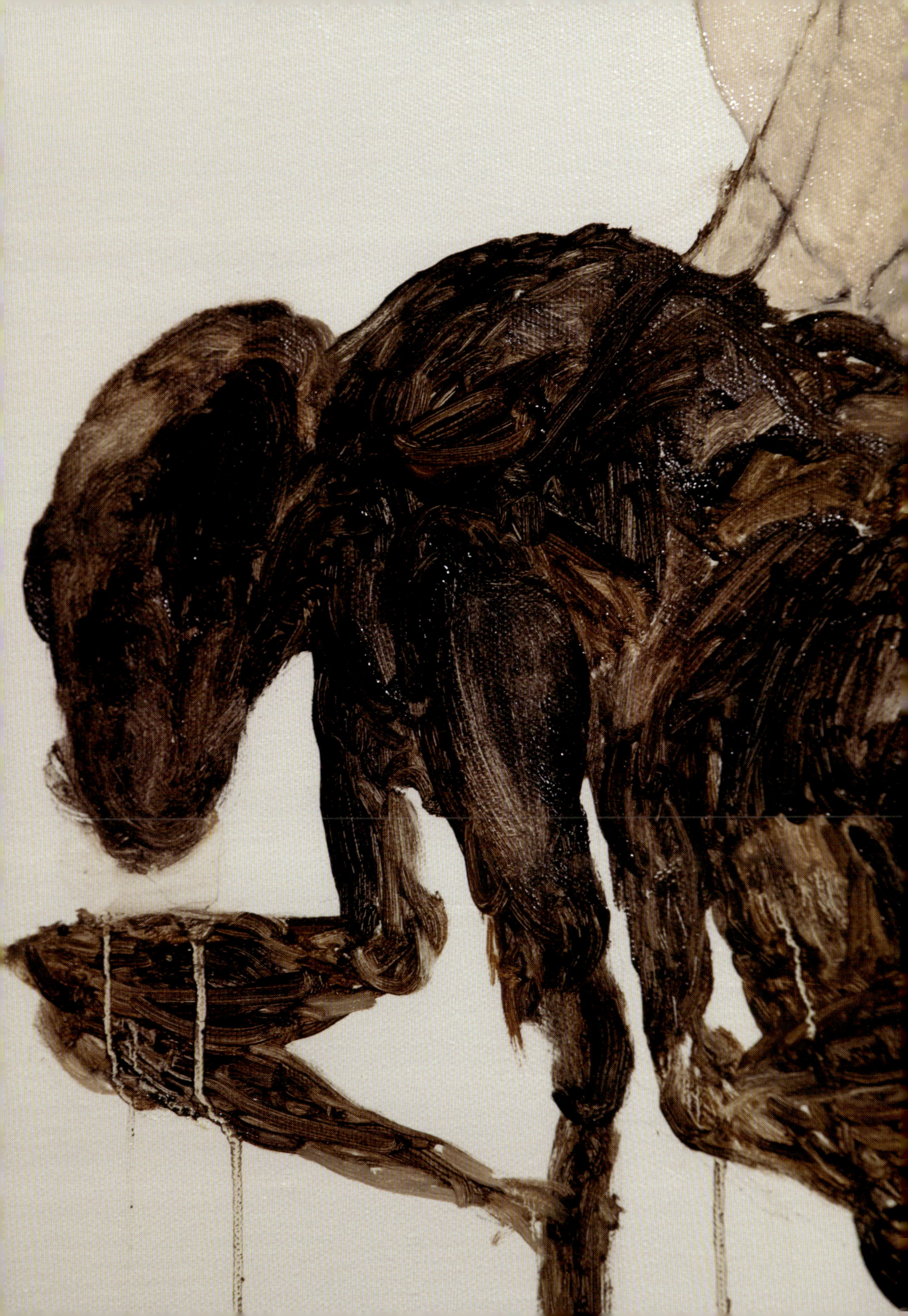

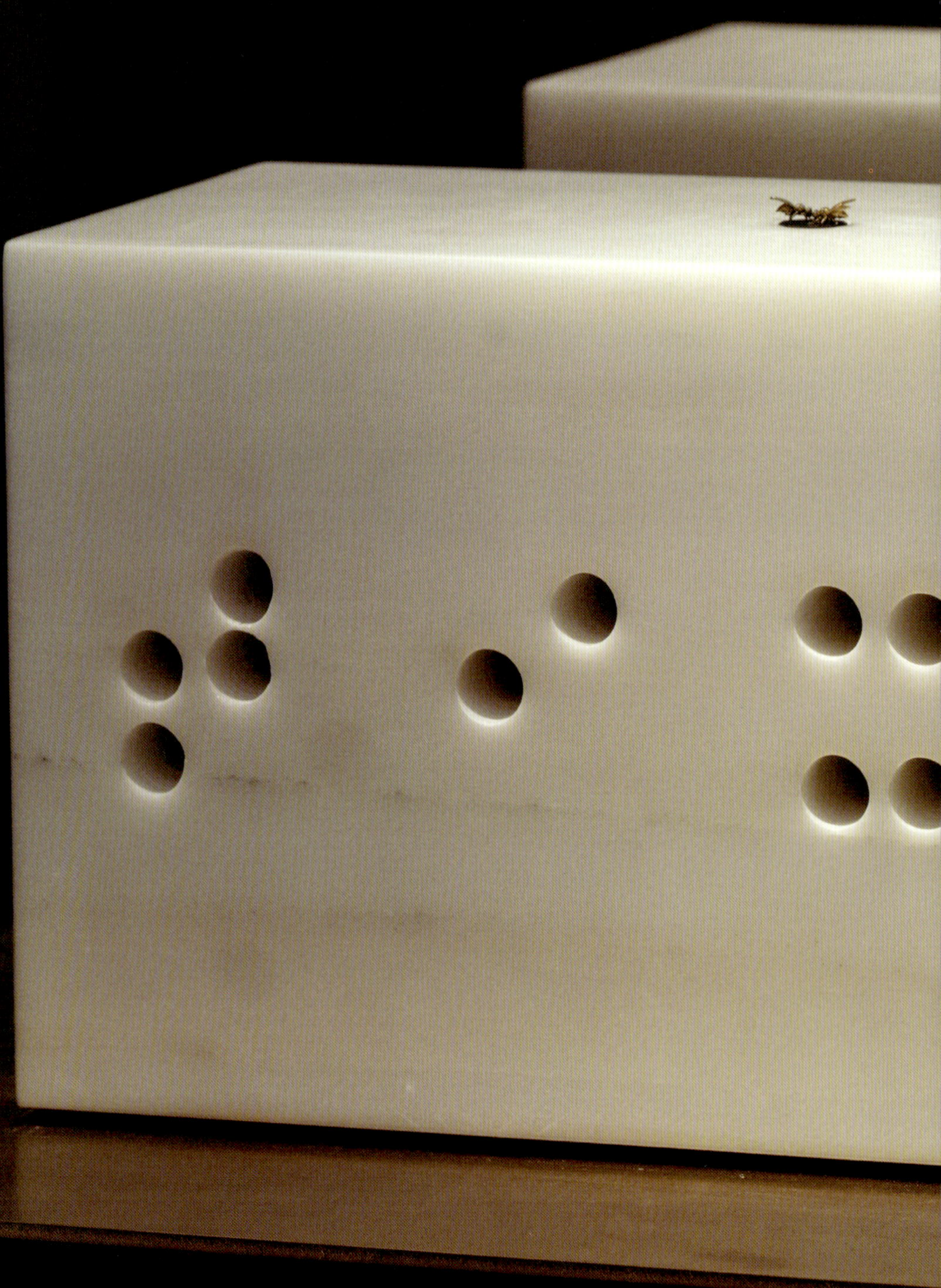

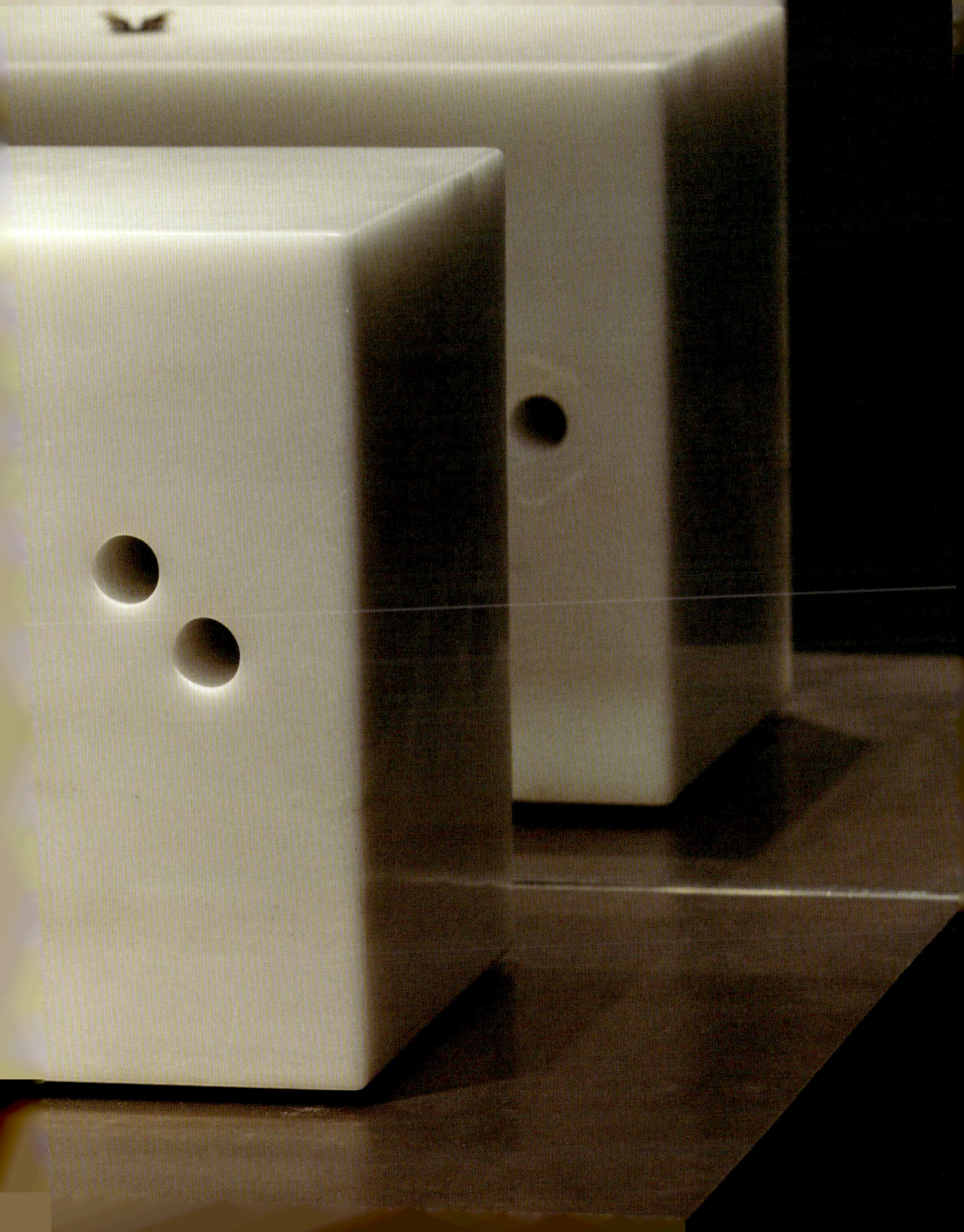

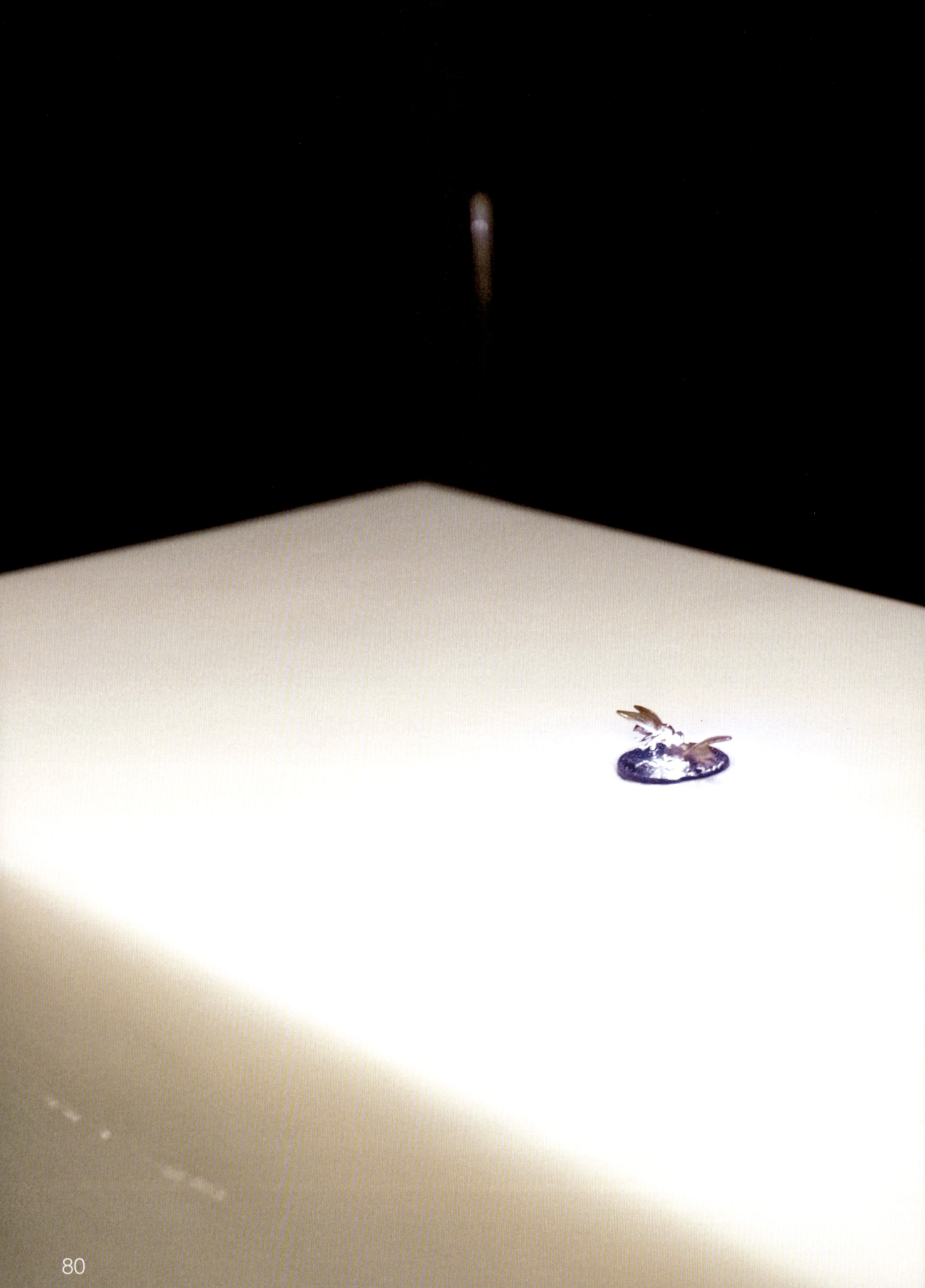

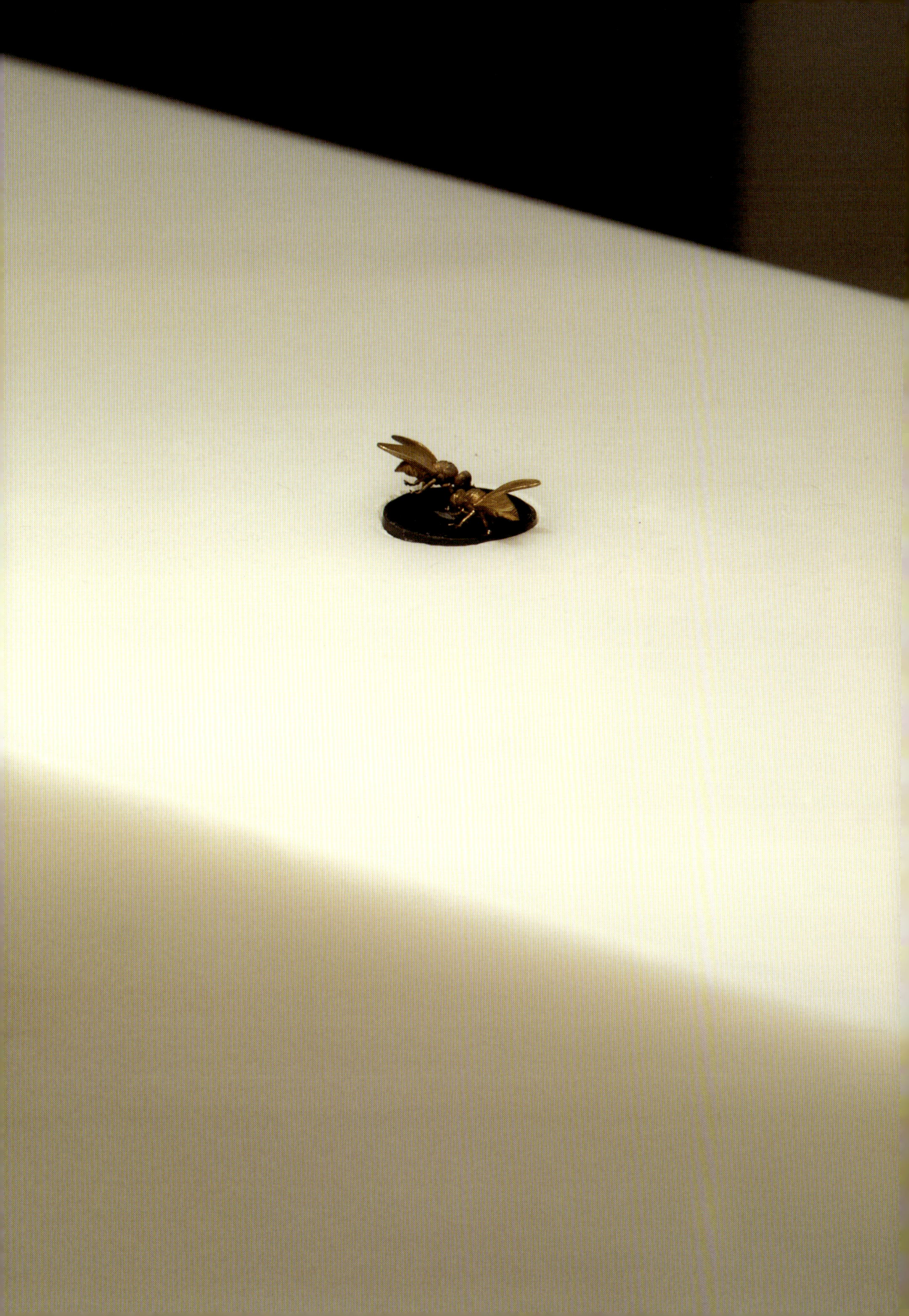

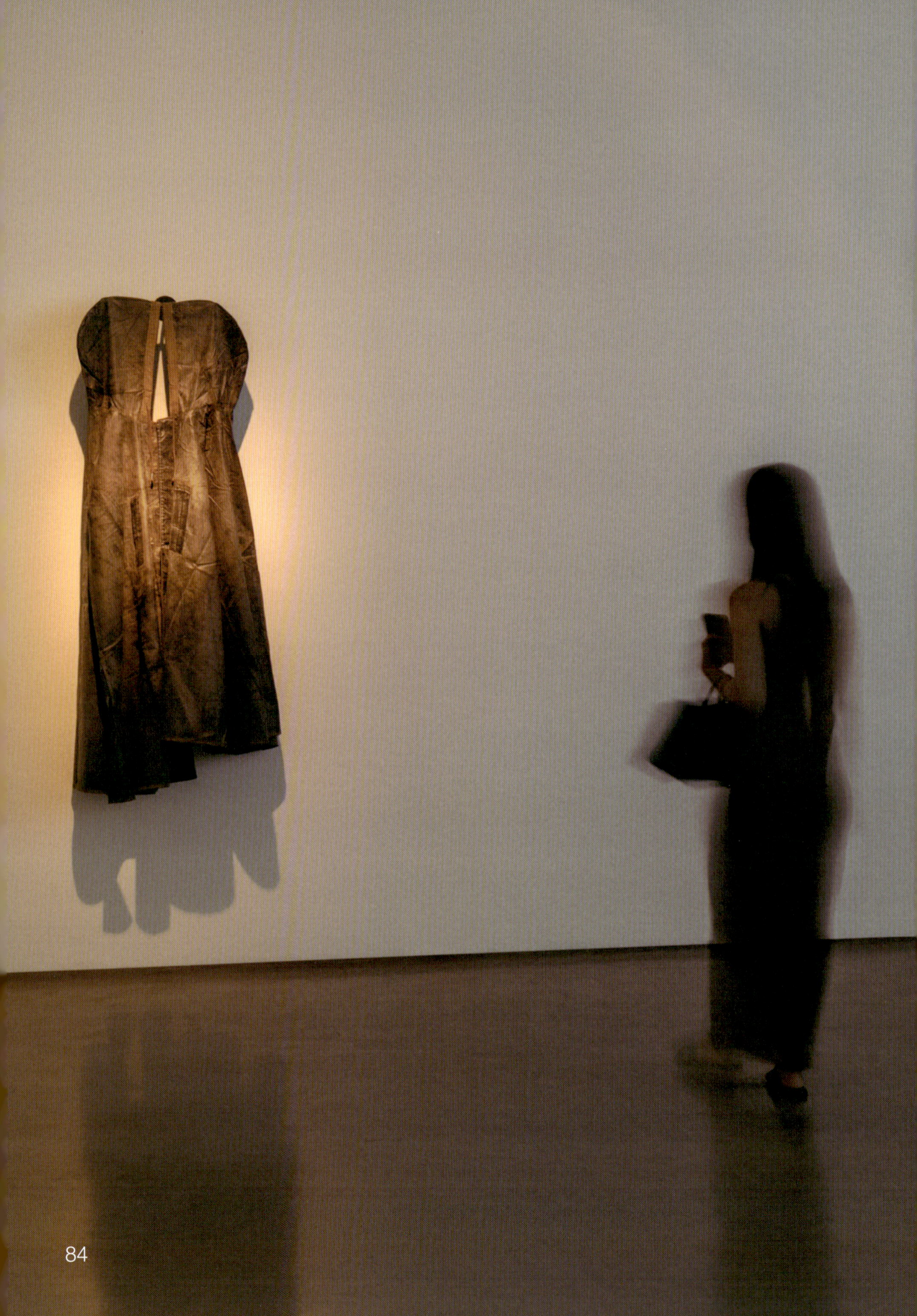

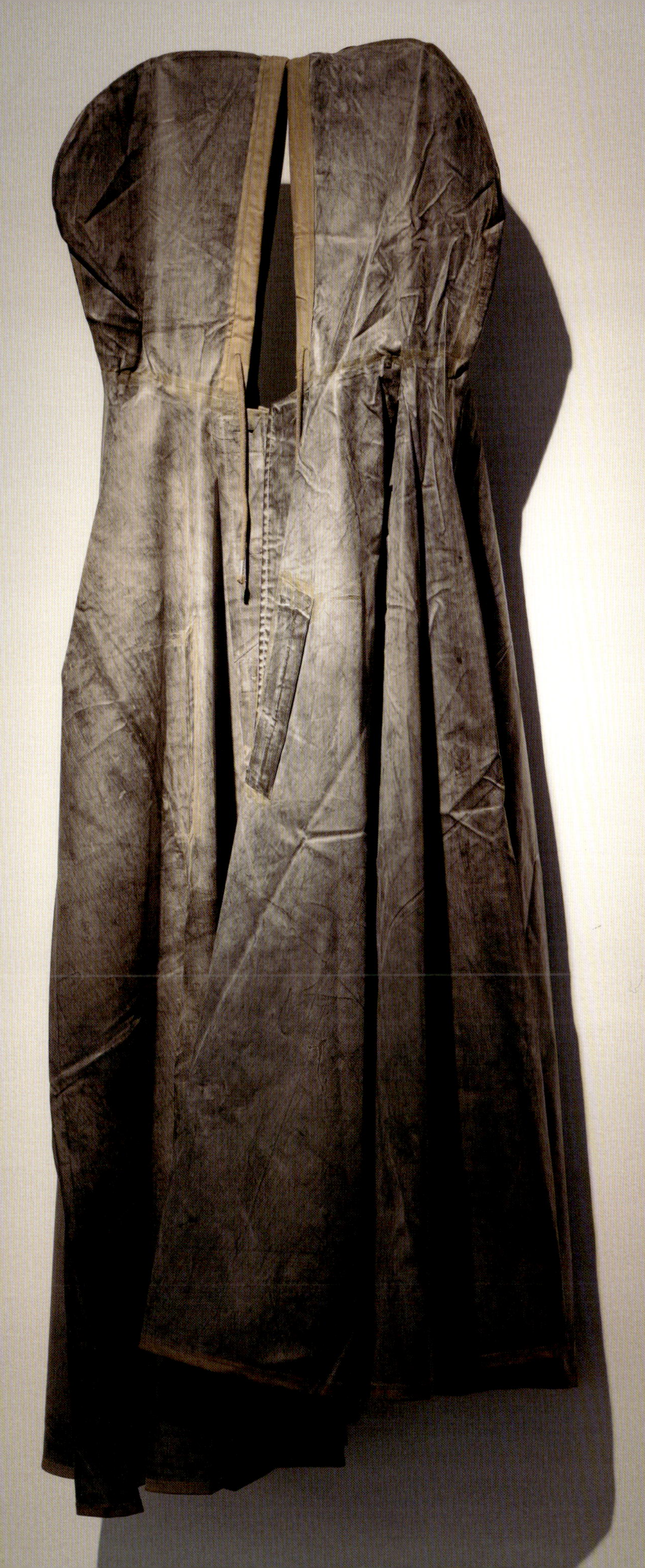

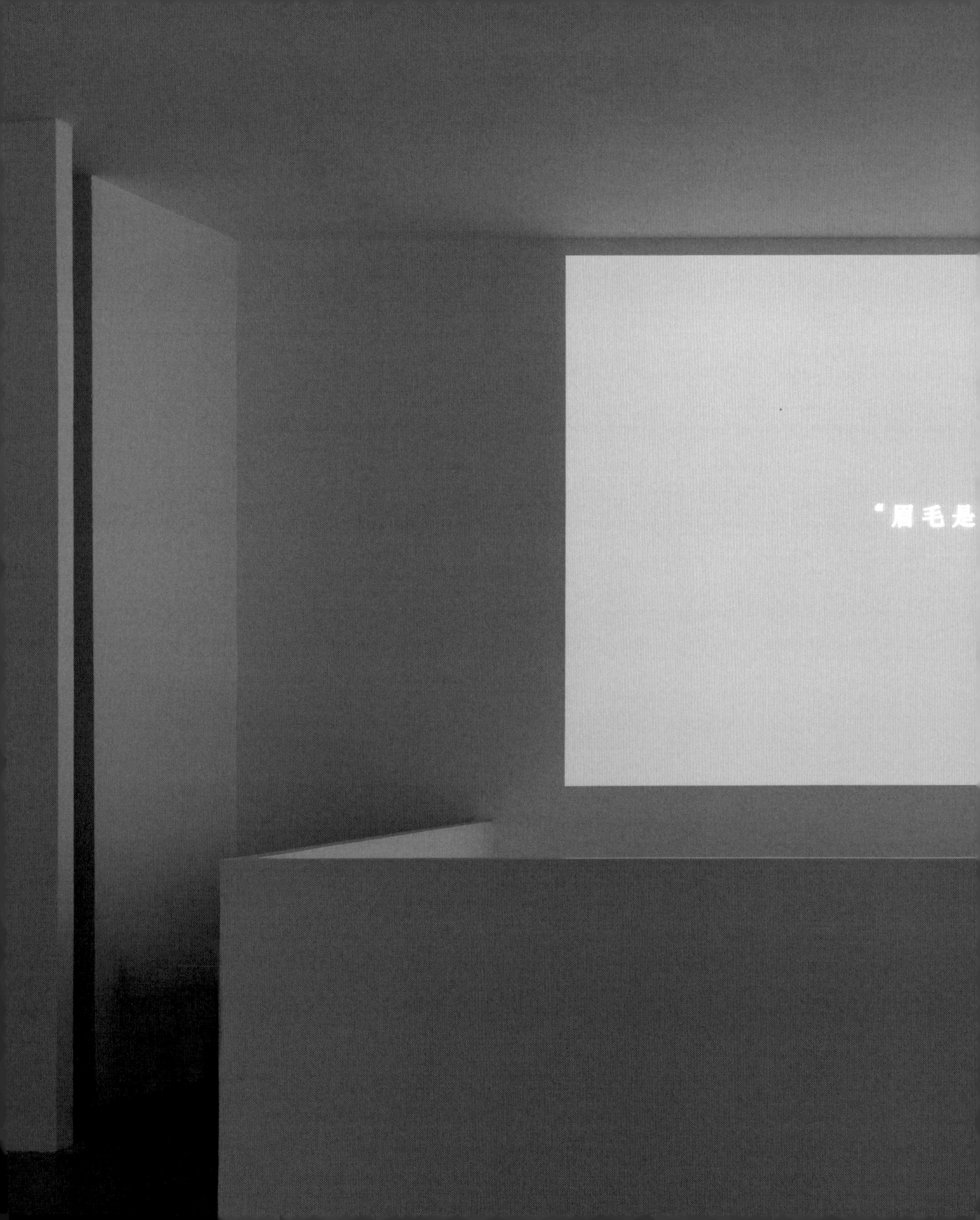
'眉毛是

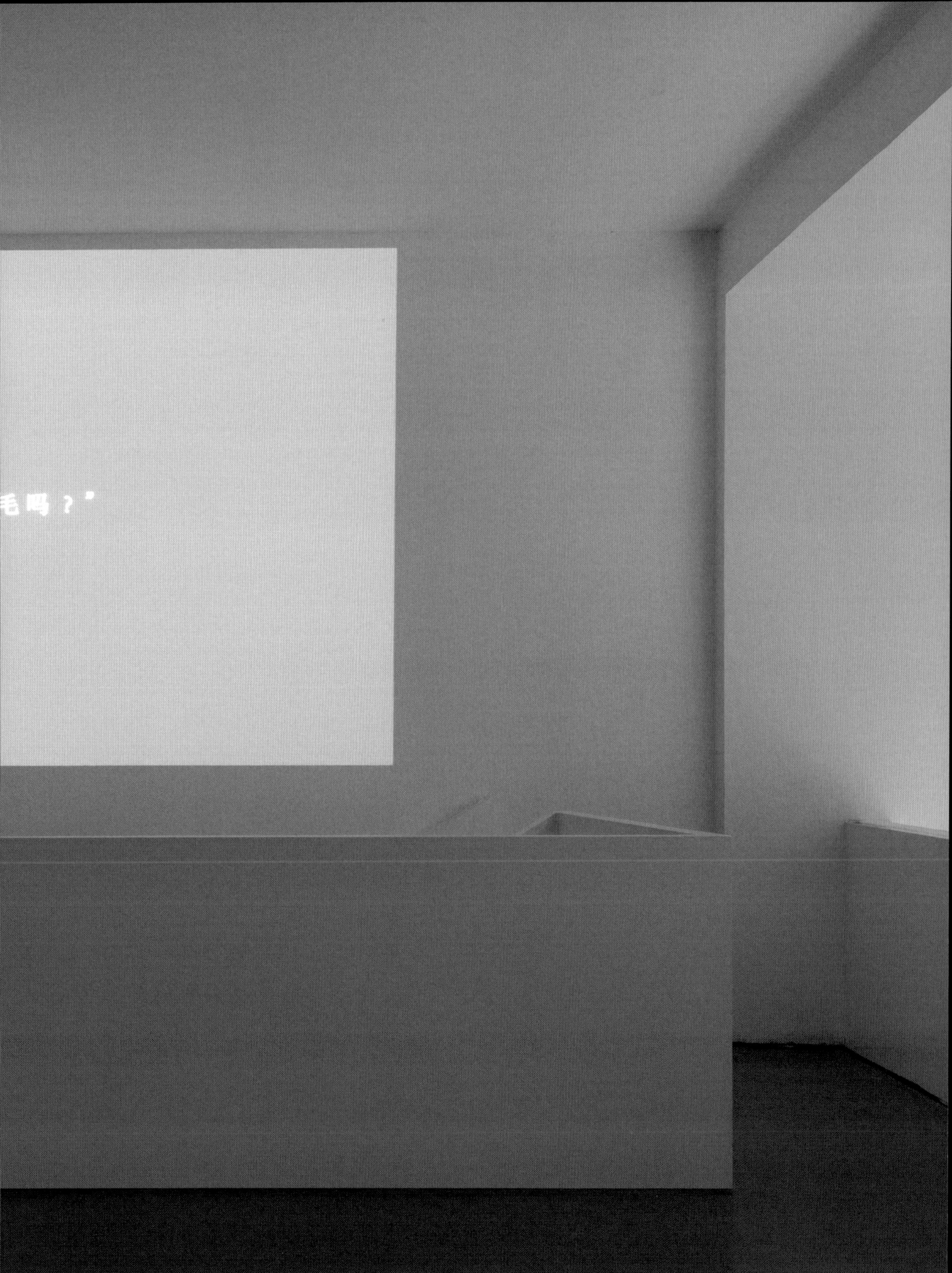
毛吗？”

List of Exhibited Works / 展览作品清单

What's the Date Today? / 今夕是何年, 2022
Stainless steel with stoving varnish / 不锈钢烤漆
780 x 632 x 5 cm
Inside back cover / 封三

Spirit on the Water / 灵在水上, 2022
Plastic chairs, glass buoys / 塑料椅, 玻璃浮标
Dimensions variable / 尺寸可变
Pages / 页 90, 91

Pillar Imperfect / 未竟之柱, 2022
White marble, aluminium, mercury, glass / 汉白玉, 铝, 水银, 玻璃
134 x 82.5 x 87.5 cm
Inside front cover / 封二; pages / 页 2–5

Thermometer / 温度计, 2022
Mercury thermometer, stainless steel with stoving varnish, copper, glass / 水银温度计, 不锈钢烤漆, 紫铜, 玻璃
30.5 x 130.5 x 5 cm
Pages / 页 4–6, 10, 11, 13

In Gold We Trust / 硬陞, 2022
Bronze, lead sheet / 青铜, 铅皮
Bronze / 青铜: 27 x 96 x 82 cm, 29 x 96 x 88 cm and / 和 23 x 92 x 87 cm;
lead sheet / 铅皮: 0.5 x 700 x 100 cm
Pages / 页 38–40

Warm/September / 但愿上天让人理解并感受到自己的和他人的愿望, 2022
Nickel chrome, silica glass / 镍铬, 石英玻璃
525 x 95 x 25 cm
Pages / 页 34–37

Waterfall / 瀑布, 2022
Beeswax, torch tip / 蜂蜡, 喷火枪头
Each / 每件 163 x 68 x 60 cm
Pages / 页 43–46, 49

Mundus / 世界, 2022
Video / 影像
04' 33"
Pages / 页 16, 17, 26, 27

Mundus / 世界, 2022
White marble / 汉白玉
103 x 103 x 70 cm
Pages / 页 14, 16, 17, 20, 21, 23–25

Mundus Is Mundus / 世界就是世界, 2022
Bronze / 青铜
33 x 33 x 1.3 cm
Cover / 封面; pages / 页 17, 32, 33; back cover / 封底

Mundus Is Mundus Is Mundus / 世界就是世界就是世界, 2022
Bronze / 青铜
99 x 99 x 1.9 cm
Pages / 页 16, 18–31

All That Is Solid Melts into Air / 一切坚固的东西都烟消云散了, 2019
Iron, electrical equipment / 钢板, 机电装置
Dimensions variable / 尺寸可变
Pages / 页 56, 57

Ball of Fat / 羊脂球, 2022
Mutton fat, copper seal, iron, glasses / 羊脂, 铜章, 铁, 玻璃
185 x 90 x 90 cm
Pages / 页 50, 51, 53, 54

If You See Her, Say Hello / 如果你看到她, 问她好, 2022
Rubber, cotton, iron / 橡胶, 棉布, 铁
Dimensions variable / 尺寸可变
Pages / 页 82–84

Asylum—1. Point, 2. King's Cross, 3. Saltpeter Is Also Philter, 4. Cloacae / 庇护所, 2022
Mixed media / 综合材料
Dimensions variable / 尺寸可变
Pages / 页 58–67

Fly / 苍蝇, 2022
Sound installation / 声音装置
Page / 页 89

Why Can't I Have Both Angels and Demons Kiss Me? / 为什么不能让天使和恶魔都亲吻我?, 2022
Oil on canvas / 布面油画
119 x 100 cm
Pages / 页 72, 74, 75

The Painful Secret of Gods and Kings / 命名是一种悲伤的行为, 2022
Bronze with polished patina, copper ore, glass / 青铜抛光, 铜矿石, 玻璃
240 x 171.5 x 63 cm
Pages / 页 68–71

Exit / 死亡是唯一的出口, 2022
White marble, bronze, gold plating, ignitor, iron, mirror / 汉白玉, 青铜镀金, 高压发生器, 铁, 镜子
135 x 56 x 30 cm
Pages / 页 73, 76–81

'Are Eyebrows Your Feathers?' / "眉毛是你的羽毛吗?", 2022
Text, screen printing and text projection / 文本, 丝网印刷及投影
Dimensions variable / 尺寸可变
Pages / 页 85, 87

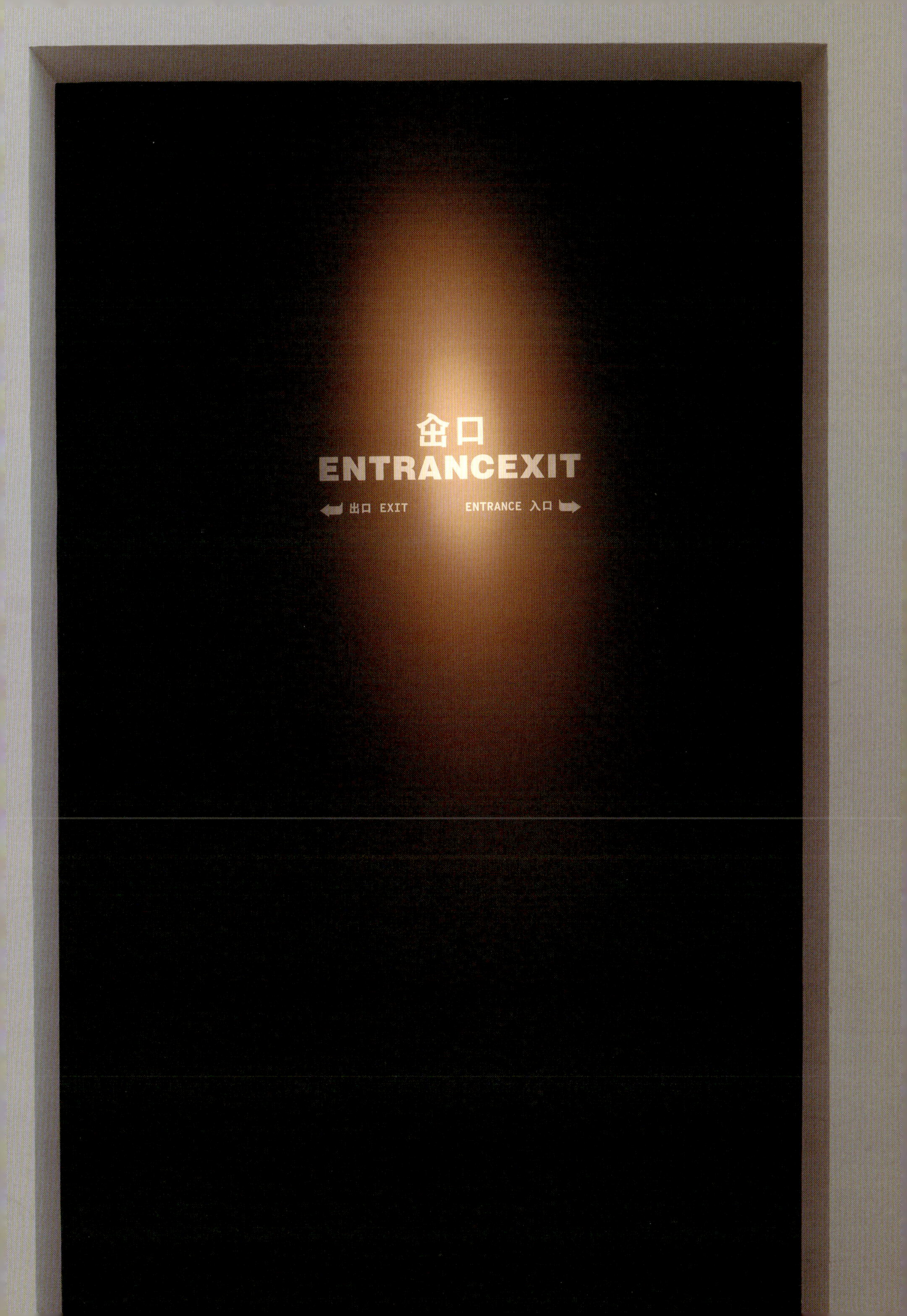

金口
ENTRANCEXIT
出口 EXIT
ENTRANCE 入口

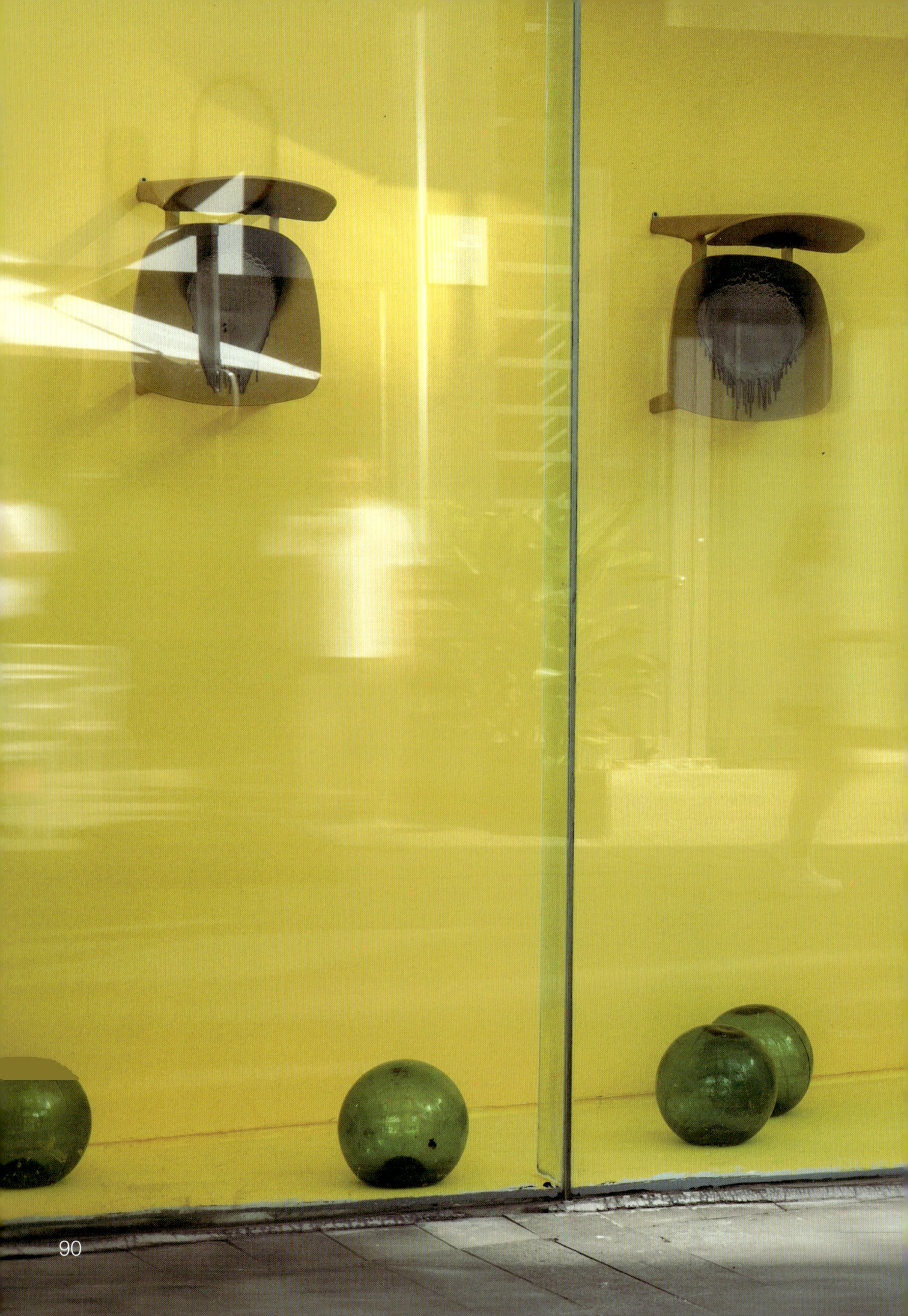

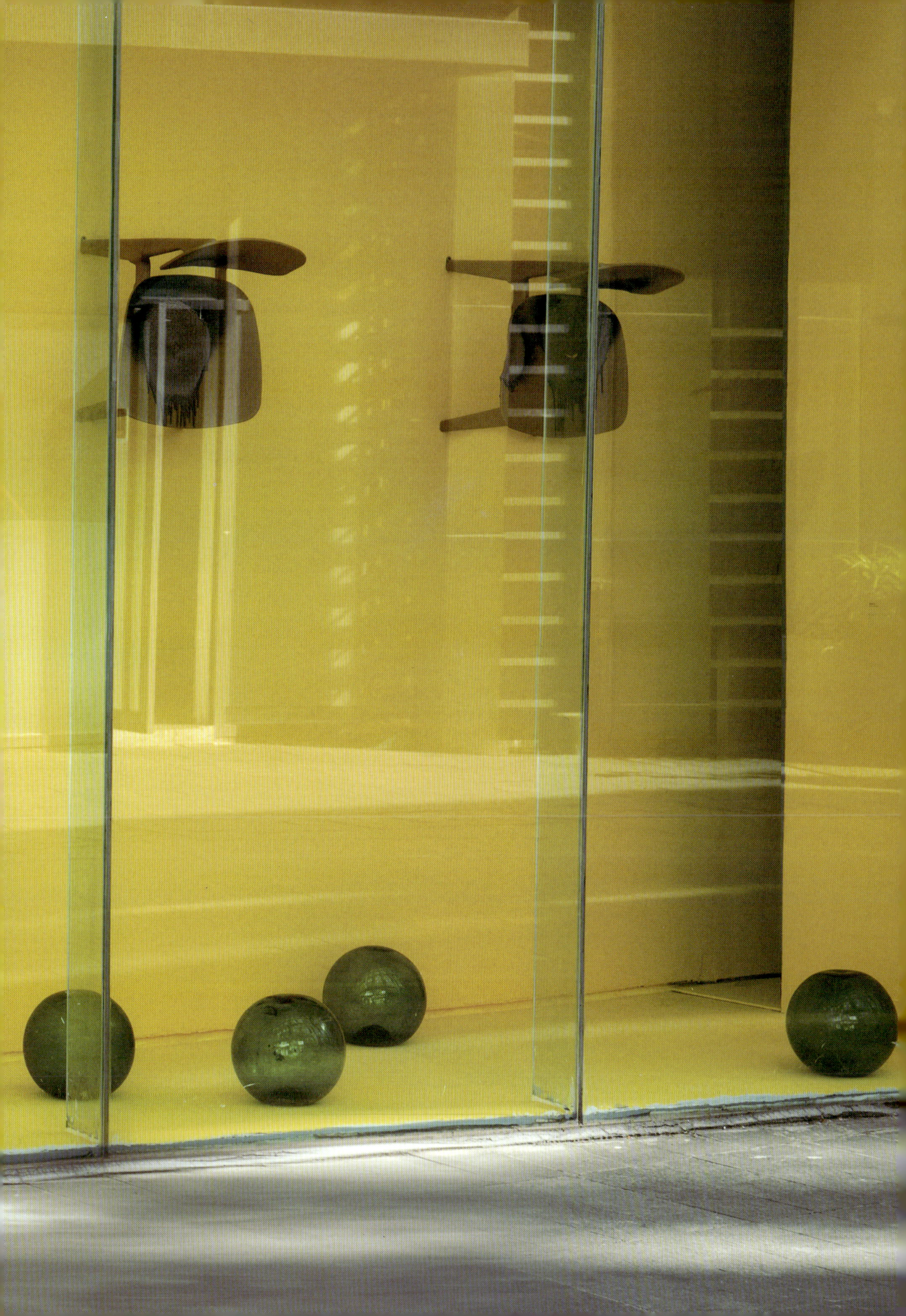